KEARNY THE MAGNIFICENT

MAJOR GENERAL PHILIP KEARNY AT WILLIAMSBURG,
May 5, 1862

KEARNY
THE MAGNIFICENT

The Story of General Philip Kearny

1815-1862

IRVING WERSTEIN

The John Day Company   New York

© 1962 BY IRVING WERSTEIN

All rights reserved. This book, or parts thereof, must not be reproduced in any form without permission. Published by The John Day Company, 62 West 45th Street, New York 36, N. Y., and simultaneously in Canada by Longmans Canada Limited, Toronto.

*Library of Congress Catalogue
Card Number: 62-10957*

MANUFACTURED IN THE UNITED STATES OF AMERICA
VAN REES PRESS • NEW YORK

In memory of Ceil who fought gallantly but lost.

ACKNOWLEDGMENTS

I wish to thank the people who helped me in preparing this book. The eminent Civil War historian, Dr. Philip Van Doren Stern, was always ready to answer my questions. The staffs of the American History Room in the New York Public Library, and the New York Historical Society gave me their traditionally courteous and efficient service.

Various members of the New York Civil War Round Table provided me with letters, diaries and journals containing material about Philip Kearny. I now thank each of them.

I found the Kearny letters in the New Jersey Historical Society, Newark, New Jersey, a treasure trove. The staff of that organization was most cooperative.

Finally, my wife was her usual patient self, and my seven-year-old son aided materially by conducting his own mysterious and wonderful doings without involving a surly author in them.

I. W.

New York City, February, 1962

PROLOGUE

Saturday, September 6, 1862

"... *mourning when their leaders fall,*
warriors wear the warrior's pall ..."

AUTUMN trespassed upon summer that year. The weather had turned brisk even before August ended, and when September came the foliage was already scarlet and russet, birds were flying south, and at sunrise the ground lay white with hoar frost. On the day of the General's funeral the autumn sun shone brightly and the air was crisp. The morning sparkled.

The tolling of church bells drifted across the New Jersey flatlands. Farmers and villagers lined the Plank Road to await the funeral procession. Only the saloons and grogshops of Newark City were open for business; all other commercial establishments had closed. The city's center was draped in mourning colors—black and purple crape hung on public buildings, stores and private homes. Even the lampposts were somber with it.

PROLOGUE

The General's portrait was in many windows—a favorite likeness showing him astride his great gray charger Moscow, his cape flying in the wind, a sword brandished in his right hand while the empty left sleeve of his tunic hung limply. On his head was the French style kepi he had always worn, cocked at a rakish angle. Spirit and courage were etched upon the face which was that of a hero. Everything about him reflected a leader whom men would follow.

"He had a quality that inspired others. In his presence cowards became lions, and weaklings—giants," a friend had once said of him.

Now the hero was dead and the people were gathered to pay him homage—those who had known him and those to whom he was only a symbol of military prowess.

But on such a day it was difficult to think long on death. Everyone wore his Sunday best, and a festive spirit soon spread among the couples strolling aimlessly, the friends stopping to chat and laugh. Young Army officers in parade uniform strutted by, stroking freshly sprouted mustaches and ogling pretty girls.

The streets were a confusion of activity. On one corner a volunteer fire department band lugubriously practiced a funeral march. A block away an Army band serenaded the people with incongruously lively military airs. An apparently tone-deaf, white-robed choir sang hymns on the steps of a church.

Every saloon was packed with customers who stood four deep at the bars. Those who could find no room inside, guzzled beer and nickel whisky on the sidewalks. A few brawls, quickly suppressed by the police, were touched off

PROLOGUE

by local hoodlums. The City Council had proclaimed that Newark's homage to the General was to be carried out "... with decorum and respect for the fallen..."

Not even the city's oldest resident could recall ever having seen such dense traffic. Buggies stood locked hub to hub with broughams; ponderous truck horses rubbed flanks with sleek carriage horses; expensive coaches were blocked by farm carts. Farm families from the surrounding countryside had come in wagons loaded with wives, children, grandmothers and grandfathers. Men swore, whips cracked, babies cried and women scolded.

Unnerved teachers of the District Free School tried desperately to keep order among the school children clutching small American flags decorated with tiny black streamers. The pupils fidgeted, shrieked, waved their flags and darted about like minnows in a pool.

A column of soldiers in seedy blue uniforms clomped around a corner and headed up Broad Street. People rushed to the curbs, pushing against police lines and crying out that the cortege had arrived. But those in front yelled back, "Don't shove! It's only the Home Guard!" A snicker went up. "Who cares about them?" someone jeered.

Home Guard companies made up of volunteers rejected by the Army for one or another reason met in the local armory once a week for drill and to perform insignificant military duties. Occasionally the Guard was called upon to patrol the railroad tracks when troop trains were due. In the unlikely circumstance that New Jersey should be invaded by the enemy it could be mustered to defend the State. A skeptical New Jersey Congressman had said of the

PROLOGUE

Guard: "They'd save the State, all right. Why, the Rebs would be so weak from laughing at the Home Guard that they'd make easy pickings."

This day the Newark Home Guard unit, mobilized to participate in the obsequies for the General, was led by a nearsighted lieutenant wearing thick glasses. The glaring sunlight made his eyes water and caused him to squint badly, but he marched with determined stride, parade sword upright against his shoulder. Behind him lumbered the men in clumsy cadence. Saloon loungers grouped on the street to mock the Home Guard. The awkward soldiers grinned sheepishly at the ridicule and plodded on, muskets canted left and right like so many pitchforks. After much milling about, the Lieutenant managed to deploy his column in two sway-backed files on opposite sides of the road. The guardsmen leaned on their bayonetted muskets, spat tobacco juice, shuffled restlessly, and exchanged quips with the crowd.

Thus, while peddlers passed through the crowds selling fruit, lemonade and candy—hawking their wares as if at the county fair grounds—the city of Newark, New Jersey, awaited the General's funeral procession.

Dressed in widow's mourning, Agnes Maxwell Kearny stood by a tall French window that overlooked the sweeping lawns of Bellegrove, the 100-acre Kearny estate situated in East Newark, a few miles from the city. A tall, slender woman with delicate features, her long auburn hair tightly drawn in a bun that hung low on her neck, she had an ethereal, fragile beauty.

PROLOGUE

From the window she could look out beyond the perfectly groomed green leaves to the placid Passaic River where a small sailboat was tacking back and forth on the sun-dappled water. A breeze stirred the scarlet-leaved maple trees along the carriage drive. A flock of sheep grazed on the grasssy slope.

Agnes listened for a moment to the voices rising from the oak-paneled parlor downstairs. That room held a wealth of memories. Each beautiful piece of furniture—each painting, figurine, vase or curio a tangible reminder of the places they had lived or visited: Paris, Rome, Vienna, St. Petersburg, Copenhagen, London. All so much a part of everything she and the General had shared—the laughter, the loving, the splendor, the tears and the sorrows.

She dreaded the ordeal yet to be faced there that morning. The burnished coffin with its silver handles and ornaments rested upon a bier. Four soldiers mounted guard beside it. Tall tapers burned at each corner of the casket. Inside were the remains of Major General Philip Kearny, aged forty-seven, late Commanding Officer, Third Division, Third Corps, Army of the Potomac, killed in action near Chantilly, Virginia, on Monday, September 1.

Agnes Kearny had perhaps always felt that her husband would be killed in battle. It was the way he had wanted to die. "I shall ride out gaily to face my fate ... with the ... cacophony of battle ringing in my ears," he had written her from the front.

Philip Kearny had known war well. He had fought against Mexicans, Indians, Arabs in Algeria and Austrian grenadiers in Italy. In 1847, on a sun-baked roadway that led to the San Antonio gate of Mexico City, he had headed a reckless cavalry charge into the muzzles of enemy cannon. A blast of grapeshot had shattered his left arm, and the limb had been amputated. But even that handicap had not kept him from war. By 1862, the daring one-armed General had become a legend among both Northern and Southern soldiers. General Winfield Scott had once said of him: "He is the bravest and most perfect soldier I have ever known."

When at home on a morning such as this he would have been out riding early, mounted on a thoroughbred stallion from his huge stable. Later he would have galloped back from the riverbank, his caracal-trimmed cape fluttering like black wings, just as Agnes had seen him a hundred times.

"Aggie! Aggie!" he would have exulted. "What an elegant day!" Anything that particularly pleased him was either "elegant" or "brilliant."

Many years later the widow recalled: "The lovely weather on the day of Phil's funeral saddened me. I remember wishing... it had been otherwise... rainy and dismal... I regretted that our Suzanne and Virginia were so young that in a few years they would no longer... have any recollection of their father... He was a man worth remembering...."

Philip Kearny had lived by his principles and ideals. He was a chivalric man, a *Beau Sabreur*. In 1861, leaving Bellegrove to join the First New Jersey Brigade, he had turned to his wife at the depot and said: "You understand that with one arm lost in Mexico I might easily have kept

PROLOGUE

out of the war, without anyone charging a want of zeal against me. But as a gentleman I felt called on to act and not be idle. Besides, I firmly believe in the Union."

This was the key to the man. A "gentleman," he felt obliged to live up to his definition of the responsibilities incumbent on that station. Others might evade danger—but not Kearny. He courted it. *"Dulce et decorum est pro patria mori"* was his motto. "It is sweet and fitting to die for one's country." This, coupled with his intense attraction for all things military, became the core of his existence.

The parlor was presently crowded with civil and military leaders; for two days, great numbers of the public had passed through for a last look at the General. Now only the funeral party occupied the room. Dress swords clanked. Spurs jingled. These were the men who would march in the cortege—colonels and majors; Senators, Congressmen; several mayors; a governor; a representative of the President of the United States, and another of the Secretary of War.

Far off in Virginia, as the funeral was about to start, the men of Kearny's division were holding a memorial service for their fallen commander. The officers and enlisted men wore black arm bands; the regimental colors were shrouded in mourning.

Agnes was startled by the chimes of a hall clock; she counted ten strokes. It was time. She went to her wardrobe and took out a black cloak and a veiled hat. After adjusting the veil and donning the cloak she glanced about the room

PROLOGUE

as though trying to remember every detail of it. In a few moments she opened the door.

From the road came the thudding of muffled drums; the troop escort was getting into line. The procession had a long way to pass—through Newark, then along the Plank Road to Jersey City. There the party was to board a crape-hung ferryboat for the trip across the Hudson River to New York City.

At the foot of Cortlandt Street a new military escort would be waiting to accompany the coffin up Broadway to Trinity Church. After the services the General was to be interred in Trinity churchyard where the Kearny family vault was located.

Agnes descended the stairs. At the bottom her husband's friend and attorney, Cortland Parker, came to her and extended his arm which she took gratefully.

Eight pallbearers carried the coffin from the house. They shuffled to an artillery caisson drawn by four matched grays, and placed the box on the gun carriage; then took positions at either side of the caisson.

Parker helped Agnes into a carriage. Six troopers from the Lincoln Cavalry troop ranged alongside the carriage, drawn sabers glistening. At the head of the column, drums ruffled; a band played a funeral march and the cortege started toward Newark. Behind the caisson an orderly led Kearny's horse Moscow, a cavalry sword hanging from the saddle pommel, empty boots in the stirrups. An infantry detachment made up of men from every regiment in Kearny's division marched at half step, rifles reversed. Sewed to the crown of each man's cap was a diamond·

PROLOGUE

shaped patch of scarlet flannel. He had personally distributed these scarlet patches.

"Wear them, boys! Wear them so the Rebels can see they're up against real fighters!" he had exhorted the troops.

Now his "boys" were following him as they had at Fair Oaks, White Oak Swamp and Malvern Hill; at Williamsburg and Chantilly. Perhaps those who marched behind his casket recalled how he had galloped up and down the battle line, reins held in his teeth, his kepi raised aloft on the tip of his sword.

"Ker-nee! Ker-nee!" they had always chanted as he swept by. "Ker-nee! Ker-nee!" they had kept shouting long after he had gone.

As her carriage rolled down the gravel driveway Agnes looked back at Bellegrove. The house with its turrets, towers and battlements had been built under Kearny's supervision. A massive bell tower topped it. From every angle the building resembled a medieval fortress. It had been modeled after a fifteenth-century castle in Saumur, France, which Kearny had admired more than twenty years before while attending the French Royal Cavalry School there. At last the carriage rounded a curve and Bellegrove was hidden by the trees.

All the way to Newark people bowed their heads as the caisson passed. Some knelt and crossed themselves; some wept. Here and there men wearing oddments of Army garb —a cap, a blouse, faded blue denim trousers—snapped to attention and saluted. A one-legged man in full uniform, yellow sergeant's stripes on his blouse sleeve, raised his cap and shouted "Good-bye, General Kearny! Good-bye!" Those standing close to him noted the scarlet patch on the crown of his cap.

When the cortege entered Newark the rampant confusion there ended abruptly. The volunteer fire department rendered its dirge. The school children stood in respectful silence. The church choir sang on key and with reverence. Even the saloon rowdies uncovered in tribute as the coffin passed by. The Home Guard came to Present Arms with such a snap that the nearsighted lieutenant gasped. The cortege wound on through Newark to the Plank Road. The drums were muffled; the bands played a slow march; the church bells tolled.

General Philip Kearny was dead.

BOOK ONE

1815–1836

"... the fiery vehemence of youth ..."

CHAPTER I

ON June 1, 1815, when the temperature soared to ninety degrees in New York City, carters' vans and private wagons piled with household goods rattled in a steady stream up Broadway, heading north to summer cottages on the shores of the Hudson and East Rivers. The houses at Kips Bay and Turtle Bay, a few miles from the Battery, were being occupied by summer residents somewhat earlier because of the unusual heat. Traffic to the wooded retreats across the river in Brooklyn was heavy, and many residents flocked to inns and cottages on Staten Island.

Anyone who could afford to do so prepared to leave the city's congested districts for the rural reaches of upper Manhattan. It was not only the heat that drove people away; the memory of the fearsome yellow-fever plague that had swept New York a decade earlier was still strong. It had started on just such a blazing June day. The epidemic survivors would never forget the terrible time. Those too young to have lived through the holocaust had heard repeated tales of the horror that had stalked New York in 1805.

By 1815, New York City had mushroomed to a population of more than 100,000 and was one of the great commercial centers of the world. Its wharves were crowded with goods destined for shipment around the globe; its harbor berthed merchant ships flying the flags of a dozen countries. From its fetid slums to its elegant homes the city teemed and throbbed with life and commerce.

Along lower Broadway, stretching from Bowling Green almost to 14th Street, stood mansions with wide lawns and extensive flower gardens. Among the most opulent of these was the great house at Number 3 Broadway. Its grounds extended westward to the Hudson River; its lawns, groves and landscaping were among the finest.

This was the property of John Watts, one of New York's wealthiest residents. His holdings included ships, mills, factories, banks and investment houses. His interests ranged throughout the world.

At sixty-six, Watts could look back upon a career of public service as well as one of mercantile success. He had been the last Royal Recorder of New York, a member of Congress after the Revolution, and for some years Speaker of the New York Legislature. But in 1808, he had abandoned politics, disgusted by the tactics of politicians. "It is as possible for a woman to preserve her chastity as it is for a man engaged in politics to retain his integrity," Watts had declared, leaving public life to devote himself to business.

Watts was an imposing man, a powerful, white-thatched, crag-faced giant whose shaggy brows hooded fierce deep-set eyes. Despite his wealth he wore simple, somber black suits, and when someone once remarked about his unstylish clothing Watts roared, "I am a gentleman, sir! Not a peacock! I do not need fine feathers!"

He was rigid and opinionated and in all his dealings brooked neither argument nor contradiction. Yet even with this arrogant nature, no man was kinder or more generous to those less fortunate. Noted for his philanthropy, Watts regarded as his monument the Leake and Watts Orphanage situated in Bloomingdale Village at the northern end of Manhattan Island. He had founded the home with a business associate, John Leake, and though he had contributed the major share of the money to establish the place, modestly requested Leake's name to be placed before his in the orphanage title.

At a time when most employers treated their workers inhumanely Watts paid his help fair wages, gave them decent housing and medical care, and set up an educational fund for their children. He lived a worthy, substantial life. Envious men said he was untouched by the trials that weighed down others, but Watts had known tragedy. He had lost his wife and three sons. The only immediate family left him was his daughter Susan who had married a handsome financier of Welsh-Irish descent—Philip Kearny

—whose own father had also married into the Watts family.

Susan's wedding reception in 1807 had created a sensation in New York. According to rumor, it had cost more than $10,000—a tremendous sum for those times. When the bridal couple returned from their European honeymoon they had moved into the spacious home Watts had built and furnished for them on land near Number 3 Broadway.

Philip Kearny had little need of his father-in-law's bounty. His father had created a large fortune as a New Jersey wine and liquor broker, and Philip himself owned a brokerage firm and maintained a 100-acre estate called Bellegrove in East Newark, plus some 10,000 acres in St. Lawrence County near Gouverneur, New York. Ten years after his marriage he became a founder of the New York Stock Exchange.

Ordinarily neither Watts nor his son-in-law would have been in New York City on June 1, 1815. The two families always left the city for St. Lawrence County at the beginning of summer. But though the city sweltered in its unseasonable hot spell, the two men waited in the library at Number 3 Broadway. Upstairs Susan Kearny writhed on a crumpled bed, wracked by birth pangs, while a worried doctor and midwife hovered over her.

A frail, delicate woman of thirty-three, Susan was twelve years younger than her husband. During the eight years of their marriage she had twice been delivered of stillborn babies, but this was proving her most difficult labor. The physician, Dr. Maurice Constantine, feared for her life.

If the two men in the library were aware of the danger, neither showed it. They waited impassively as rain clouds gathered and thunder growled sullenly over stifling Manhattan. The day passed and the night brought no change in the temperature, although the promise of rain was still audible. As darkness fell a servant came to light the lamps. A cold supper was wheeled in. When the meal was over each puffed meditatively on his cigar. Each was wrapped in his own thoughts.

Perhaps John Watts was remembering an earlier time when he had waited in this room for a life or death verdict. It had been during the Great Plague. His wife—another Susan—and his son John were ill with the fever.

The night was hot but the windows had been sealed against the polluted outside air. In the streets one could smell death despite the sulphur torches that spluttered on every lamppost. Health authorities believed that they purified the air. The noxious sulphur fumes permeated the house; not only had the odors seeped in from outside, but sulphur candles burned in every room. To no avail. Susan and John had died before morning.

All that ghastly summer the hearses rolled past and death notices filled columns in the newspapers; the yellow-fever epidemic of 1805 was a devastating one.

Watts had stayed in the city the entire summer, going into those sections most severely affected by the plague to help their victims with money and medicines. He exposed himself to contagion recklessly, but did not contact the disease even through the worst stages of the outbreak. "I began to believe that the Almighty was sparing me ... for some purpose which he had not yet chosen to reveal," Watts said later.

With the onset of cool weather in September the epidemic had waned. Early frost nipped the breeding grounds of the disease-bearing mosquitoes in the Jersey flats. The nightmare ended. New Yorkers returned to their homes, and as the brisk weather continued the city had a revival of spirits.

Water carts sprinkled the streets and wet cobblestones glistened in the sunshine. Housemaids in starched caps and aprons polished corroded brass doorknobs, scrubbed stone stoops, and washed windows until the houses gleamed. Everyone worked to erase the stains of the dreadful summer. Even the mean slum streets assumed a brighter aspect, although nothing could really change those bleak neighborhoods.

Sweet-potato vendors appeared on the streets again. Hot-corn sellers returned, and the chestnut man trundled his wheeled charcoal brazier up one street and down another, chanting "Hot chestnuts! Hot! Hot! Hot!" Ragged match girls peddled sulphur matches to the theatregoers who crowded Fulton Street. Thugs mugged drunken sailors on the water front. A nasty riot erupted at City Hall between rival gangs. A tenement in the Five Points slum burned to the ground while two rival volunteer fire companies fought with hose nozzles and spanners for possession of the one street hydrant.

The city was back to normal.

John Watts had groped his way back too. At first, after the epidemic had passed, he seldom left his house, but sat locked in his library, leafing through a book or staring through the windows. The deaths of Susan and John had reawakened his grief for the two sons who had died a few years earlier. Robert and Charles had been sailing on the East River when a sudden squall overturned their boat and both had drowned.

Watts grew increasingly withdrawn and austere. Still, he saw life going on about him every day through his library windows; people hurried up and down Broadway, each occupied with his own affairs. To John Watts they were only nameless strangers, yet through watching them he began to realize that he could not resign from the world and live wrapped in his own grief. He had been indulging in self-pity—a quality he had always despised. If his wife and sons were dead, his daughter Susan still lived—and needed him.

At that time Susan, a gentle young woman of twenty-three, was still unmarried and—notwithstanding her father's fortune—without suitors. Society gossips predicted she would die a spinster. "The girl's a mouse. No man wants to marry a woman afraid of her own shadow, even if she does have the wealth of a Croesus," a socialite matron sneered.

John Watts made up his mind that Susan would marry. He vowed to find her a husband— "... the best match in town..." he promised.

Once John Watts decided on something it was usually done. In his quest for a proper son-in-law he took Susan with him on an inspection tour of his holdings in England, France and Italy. In Rome he arranged for his daughter to meet Philip Kearny. The handsome financier had captured Susan's heart, just as her father had planned.

Now Watts flicked the ashes from his cigar. A shudder ran through him. He was afraid that Susan was going to die. Perhaps at that moment he wondered what he would do if she died and the baby lived. Suppose he were to have to make a choice between the mother and child? Which would it be? The new life for the old? The old for the new? Tears welled in his eyes and suddenly Watts felt old and tired.

Philip Kearny lounged in a deep leather chair on the opposite side of the room. Outwardly he seemed unruffled, but his eyes nervously searched the room: the familiar book-lined walls, the huge fireplace, the full-length portrait over the mantel of a youthful John Watts in the robes of the Royal Recorder. On another wall hung a portrait of his mother-in-law as a young bride; the resemblance to his Susan was startling.

Life had been fairly untroubled for Kearny. Born wealthy, he was well educated and had attended the best schools. After graduating from Harvard College he had spent a year at the Sorbonne and another year roaming about Europe. Urbane, sophisticated and traveled, Kearny was the prototype of an upper-class New Yorker.

He had married Susan Watts when he was thirty-five. The marriage was a good one. He had known many women before, but all that was over. Kearny was a hedonist, not a philanderer. He loved Susan and respected her. Only the lack of a child marred their marriage. He wanted a son to succeed him in business.

After the two stillborn boys, Susan had been warned that another child might prove fatal, but she had pledged Doctor Constantine to secrecy about her condition, and it had been only a few days ago that the husband and father had learned of it.

Although Kearny gave the impression of calmness he was torn and heartsick. But because he believed that a gentleman should never reveal his emotions, his apprehensions were masked. Perhaps he found the situation ironical. He had unlimited money, prestige and influence—none of which could do anything to save Susan and his child. In this—at this moment in time—he was as helpless as a chimney sweep.

At 10 P.M. the rainstorm broke upon the city. It came in a deluge heralded by a monstrous streak of lightning and a violent thunderclap. A gusty westerly wind moaned across Manhattan. The pelting rain churned dirt roadways into viscous mud. Small cataracts rushed down paved streets. The wind raised whitecaps in the harbor, and as it gained in intensity lashed the water into giant waves. Anchored ships strained at their moorings and several broke loose to wallow in the heaving sea.

The storm proved to be one of the most severe in years. The wind wrenched shutters loose; rain rattled like buckshot against the windows; cellars were flooded, and the torrent swept away squatters' shacks along the banks of the East River. Rooftops were blown off; walls fell in; trees toppled. A tenement on Front Street collapsed, killing a dozen persons.

In the Watts house all was safe and snug, but the storm outside matched the growing intensity in the library as the hours passed. Watts paced the room, hands clasped behind his back. His imperiousness had vanished; now he was merely a worried and frightened old man.

It was almost midnight when fat, ruddy Dr. Constantine came into the room, his grenadier's mustache bristling, his silver-framed eyeglasses glinting in the lamplight. Beaming at the anxious men like a plump tomcat, he chuckled.

"It's a boy! A healthy boy, and I believe the mother is fine."

Watts rang for champagne and offered a toast to the grandson who would be named Philip Kearny, Junior. It was a family tradition that the first son bear the name of Philip.

As the three men sipped their wine in the Watts library, waves smashed against the old sea wall at the Battery. A sloop was pounded into splinters off Hell Gate. The storm spread havoc throughout the island.

No one in the Watts house could foresee that the furious storm may have symbolized the baby's future. His life was fated to be as tumultuous and violent. Born in a storm, he was destined to die on a night as turbulent as the one in which he had entered the world.

Near daybreak the rain abated and the wind diminished; the storm passed out to sea before dawn. Bodies of drowned sailors bobbled in the rivers. Volunteers searching for victims dug in the wreckage of the ruined Front Street tenement. Two gangs of river pirates fought with knives and brass knuckles for the salvage rights to a grounded schooner.

A light flickered in an upstairs room at Number 3 Broadway. The newborn baby mewled peevishly while his mother slept.

The long night was ended.

CHAPTER II

IN 1823, when Philip Kearny, Junior was eight, he came in contact with death for the first time. That meeting came on a mild afternoon during the last week of March. The touch of spring was apparent everywhere. Lawns were greening, crocuses poked cheerfully out of the damp earth, and trees showed buds. Along the riverbank, close to the shore line, minnows darted, and at night when mist lay on the water young Phil could hear the bullfrogs calling *"Gerunk! Gerunk!"* among the marsh reeds.

The winter was over and the boy was glad. Soon it would be summer which meant moving to the family country place at Gouverneur. Summertime was horseback riding across wide fields, hoofs pounding on the old plank bridge that spanned the Oswegatchie River where it crossed

Kearny land. Although only eight, Phil was a good rider and could keep up with almost any grown man. This ability of his grandson pleased John Watts, himself a magnificent horseman. Summer brought swimming and camping trips in the Adirondacks which loomed blue and purple on the horizon to form a three-sided backdrop for the rolling acres of the Kearny estate.

Philip went to school at Ufford's Academy, reputed to be the "finest institution of learning specializing in the education of genteel boys." The academy's roster carried an impressive list of family names, and Cyril Ufford—a prissy, spindly legged pedant—flitted from class to class supervising a curriculum that included: "... the studies of mathematics, history, geography, Latin, French, penmanship, composition, drawing, etiquette and gentlemanly comportment...."

Ufford's pupils were largely pampered boys who displayed little academic promise. Young Phil was no exception, although he excelled in drawing pictures of soldiers and horses. His notebooks were crammed with imaginative battle scenes of charging infantry and galloping cavalry rather than lessons. If he could not do a simple arithmetic sum, at least he won high praise from his drawingmaster.

When the spring semester of 1823 was ending, Kearny, Senior received his son's term report. The marks were so low in every subject except drawing that the father exploded. "I have no intention of raising a harebrained artist! You are done with Ufford's, young man. I shall send you to a school where scholarship and discipline are stressed."

He enrolled his son at the Round Hill School in Northampton, Massachusetts, for the fall term. That school was noted for its academic level and strict discipline. But even before young Kearny left Ufford's he suffered a shattering loss.

He was accompanied to school every day by the Kearny butler Peter, a dignified Negro who also called for him when the sessions were over. One day in March, Peter appeared at the school before dismissal time. Little Philip was taken from class, and Peter took his hand and strode quickly up Broadway toward the Kearny house. The youngster trotted anxiously beside him.

"What's the matter, Peter?" he gasped.

The butler marched on silently until they were a block from the house, when he stopped and gazed at the frightened boy looking up at him.

"Master Phil," the butler murmured, "Master Phil, you have to be brave. Your mamma is dead."

Twenty years later Kearny remembered: "I can recall that terrible moment with unusual clarity. I can still hear Peter's words . . . telling me that I had lost my beautiful, wonderful mother forever . . ."

Susan Kearny had never fully recovered from her last ordeal of childbearing and was often confined to her bed for days at a time. Despite Dr. Constantine's optimistic predictions, she grew steadily weaker. A parade of doctors filed in and out of her room, whispering together, frowning and looking wise. Some prescribed galvanic treatments; others called for leechings and cuppings. They compounded tonics and blood purifiers of foul-smelling herbs. Quacks with weird remedies entered briefly and departed.

John Watts took his daughter to Germany for the mineral waters and sulphur baths at Aachen and Baden-Baden with no success; Susan grew steadily weaker. But her nature never changed. She was always gentle and even tempered and never complained.

On sunny days when she felt well enough she would lie in a wicker lounge chair on the lawn beside the house, facing the river. Philip liked those times the best and spent hours keeping his mother company and playing in the grass. Sometimes he was a savage warrior creeping through the bushes and leaping out at her with a chilling war whoop. She would cry out in mock terror and then burst into delighted laughter.

Often she read to him or told him stories of the time when knights rode forth on quests. She taught him about chivalry; about ancient heroes such as Horatius and Leonidas; and about American heroes—Nathan Hale, "Mad Anthony" Wayne, Ethan Allen and "Swamp Fox" Marion. She told him of explorers and adventurers, ships' captains and pirates. He sat huddled at her feet, wide eyed, hugging his knees with all the strength in his frail arms.

As a boy Kearny was thin, small boned and delicately built. Dr. Joseph G. Cogswell of the Round Hill School described him: ". . . he was a sensitive dark-eyed youngster, strikingly handsome and with a most engaging manner . . ."

Philip was close to his mother because she understood him better than anyone else. Susan worried about his school work and agreed with her husband that Ufford's was not the place for him, but silently suffered grave anxieties about sending him away from home to Round Hill.

She could have spared herself the worry, for she died in her sleep, unaware and without pain, in that spring season when life was again surging all about. She had loved the springtime.

The bereaved boy missed his mother. He withdrew into a shell where no one could reach him. The weeks dragged by and the school term ended in mid-May. On June 1, his eighth birthday, Phil was at his father's house in Gouverneur with John Watts and a staff of servants. The cook baked a cake for the solemn eight year old, and Watts gave him a full-blooded colt. The boy's only response to the gift was a polite "Thank you" and a dutiful peck on his grandfather's cheek.

Several days later his father came up from New York and the three went riding together. Philip was mounted on his new colt which he had named Tarquin. He jogged along next to his father while John Watts brought up the rear. They went deep into the woods and came upon a disused logging road which was bumpy and full of potholes, making it a dangerous place for a horse.

Suddenly Phil cried out, "I wonder how fast Tarquin can run!"

The elder Kearny smiled. "Surely you don't mean to try him here?"

"Why not, Father? I'll find out now. Right now!" his son exclaimed, and just as John Watts rode up, the impetuous boy spurred Tarquin into a gallop and raced down the trail.

"Come back!" his father shouted.

"Stop him! He'll break his neck!" Watts cried.

"It's no use, I'd never catch that colt," Kearny, Senior said. "No one could."

"You're right. Oh, the little fool..." Watts moaned.

Kearny, Senior recalled: "We had to watch helplessly... in horrified fascination as Phil spurred the colt even faster..."

The animal seemed to be skimming the ground, his black coat shining with sweat. Watts and Kearny knew that a single misstep could prove fatal to both horse and rider.

The boy rode low in the saddle, pressed against Tarquin's neck "like a jockey in a steeplechase," as his father said later. Phil guided the colt deftly and with skill. After riding at a breakneck pace for nearly a mile he turned Tarquin about and trotted back to his anxious father and grandfather. By the time he reached them both had regained their composure.

The elder Kearny eyed him coldly. "Go back to the house at once!" he ordered.

"Yes, Father," his son said. "I don't care how you punish me. That ride was grand! It was worth anything!" He wheeled the colt and rode off toward the house.

John Watts chuckled. "The rascal. The skinny little rascal. Did you ever see such riding, and over such ground? That boy is made of the right stuff. Eight years old and riding like that! He has courage. Real courage!"

Watts repeated the story of the ride to anyone who would listen, and since few dared not pay attention when he spoke, the tale soon spread through the village. Whenever

Philip galloped into Gouverneur, heads turned to watch him. Even the old men sunning on the porch of the general store stopped whittling long enough to stare after him.

"That youngster'll ride to his death one day," a local character predicted.

CHAPTER III

THE boyhood years slipped away and before anyone realized how much time had passed Phil Kearny was fifteen years old. A tall, graceful youth, he had a lean, wiry body and black eyes that smoldered in his handsome, patrician face.

His stay at Round Hill School had ended in May, 1830, when he transferred to Highland Academy at Cold Spring, New York, directly across the Hudson from West Point. Of the time he spent at Round Hill Dr. Cogswell wrote: "Kearny was remarkable for his gentle and amiable character ... took high rank as a scholar, and was greatly beloved as a pupil."

Philip spent his vacations at Gouverneur but had not returned until late July this year because of special classes he had been taking at Highland. He was glad to be back.

The house, built on a rise overlooking the village, was large and comfortable. It was splendidly located and commanded a sweeping view in every direction. Herds of cattle grazed on Kearny pastureland; fields abounded in midsummer crops; the orchards were laden with ripening fruit; wheat, corn and barley grew high.

To the west, beyond rows of waving, tasseled corn, the Oswegatchie River coiled like a sleepy snake. Southward a branch of the river wound through Hailesboro, turned suddenly north, and wandered to the east to empty into Cranberry Lake some thirty miles away. On Kearny property the Oswegatchie raced through a twenty-foot-deep rocky gorge crossed by an old wooden bridge.

By the time Philip arrived the house was filled with summer guests. Friends and relatives occupied the bedrooms; children romped on the lawns. The cookhouse was redolent with roasting turkeys, ducks, geese and chickens. Spicy hams, sides of bacon and strings of sausage hung in the smokehouse. Tubs of rich, yellow butter and gallons of sweet milk and cream crammed the icehouse. A deep cellar vault was dusty with tiers of bottles of imported and domestic wines.

Philip Kearny, Senior lived in a style to be expected of the owner of such an estate. His guests included De Peysters, Van Rensselaers, Delanceys, Schermerhorns, Gansevoorts and Schuylers. Each evening saw a score or more ringed about the long oak table in the Kearny dining room —the size of a baron's great hall. Few of even the most ambitious New York hostesses could have gathered so many prominent names under one roof at the same time.

Kearny was a skillful host. On occasion he surrendered his place at the head of the table to John Watts when the old man felt well enough. Watts was now eighty-one years of age. His craggy face had grown flabby, his penetrating eyes were sometimes lackluster, and occasionally he lost his trend of thought. But no one considered him senile. When necessary he could muster all his one-time wit, sharpness and shrewdness.

Much had changed in fifteen years. Number 3 Broadway no longer stood as an opulent oasis in the city. New York was greatly altered. Commercial establishments had crept from the Battery northward until shops, offices and countinghouses blighted Broadway as far as Canal Street and beyond. Between that street and the Battery scarcely a single private residence faced on Broadway. Many homes had been demolished and replaced by ugly red-brick buildings. Street paving and cobblestones covered the once verdant lawns. Now clerks and mechanics walked where the wealthy gentry had strolled.

John Watts was not one to be ruled by sentimentality. He knew the tide could not be halted. The days of gracious living in that part of the city were over. His house at Number 3 had meant a great deal to him. His children—and his grandson—had been born in it; his wife and son had died there. But this was part of an era drawing to its close. In 1825, Watts sold the house and land and persuaded Kearny to do the same with his property. Both realized large profits on the sales.

Watts owned real estate farther uptown at 22nd Street,

with boundaries that streched from Fourth Avenue to the Hudson River. As yet the streets appeared only as grids on maps, for the city had not been laid out that far north and the area was still pleasantly rural. On this property, some years earlier, Watts had built a house called Rose Hill which stood on a slope where rambler roses bloomed in profusion. After selling Number 3, Watts moved to Rose Hill. His widower son-in-law came to live with him, now that young Phil was away at school. When the youth returned to New York for Easter or Christmas holidays he stayed at Rose Hill. He was fond of that part of the city and spent hours roaming in the nearby woods.

Young Kearny's childhood had been a lonely one. The death of his mother had taken from him the only real love in his life. Now he received every material advantage, but neither warmth nor understanding. His grandfather was a patriarch—a man to respect, but a figure too grand for a boy to love. His father was completely engrossed in business and had little time to spare his son. A man of power and prestige in the financial world, Kearny had apparently never considered remarrying.

He, too, gave the boy all the material benefits of money. At Gouverneur, Phil had a string of his own thoroughbred horses. An Italian fencing master was hired to coach him in foil and saber. A British middleweight boxer taught him to use his fists. His riding instructor was a former French cavalry captain. He had a tutor for dancing, another for etiquette. At fifteen the younger Kearny had all the manners, comportment and social poise of a wealthy young aristocrat.

His father had molded him carefully, but had neglected the one ingredient needed to make him a whole person; Kearny had given his son everything except affection.

Young Philip was expected to achieve the standards set for him by his father and grandfather. Often he must have wanted to tell Kearny, Senior that he could not attain some of the goals he was being asked to reach. But he did not have that sort of frank relationship with his father. In fact he seldom saw him except at mealtimes and then merely to exchange polite conversation, as though with a stranger.

The boy was proud and reserved and had few intimates, preferring to be alone much of the time. At Round Hill School, although liked by everyone, he made no close friends.

A cousin, John Watts De Peyster, who did become his closest associate, noted: "In his choice of friends ... Phil was regulated by his own arbitrary rules of what they should be rather than what they were. He selected them with all the coolness of maturer age ... for qualities which suited his prejudices ... and these extended to almost everything ... He was fond of clothes ... exceedingly neat and careful of his person, and always affected a sort of military carriage or a touch of something military in his costume ... He was pleased to hear someone say of him, 'There goes a soldier in civil dress....'"

Philip was completely fascinated by the military. His uncle Stephen Watts Kearny, a Major in the regular Army, was regarded as one of the country's outstanding officers. According to rumor, the Major—a hero of the War of 1812—was slated for high command; some said he was being groomed as Commander in Chief of the Army. Young Kearny had not only the example of his Uncle Stephen to follow but also a line of blood relatives who had won military fame in various American wars. Kearnys had fought in the Revolution, the War of 1812 and the Seminole War. During the Revolution many in the clan had been Tories serving the King against their kinsmen.

Philip revealed to De Peyster his desire for a military career. It was this ambition which sparked a crisis that flared between the youth and his father during the summer of 1830.

The boy was imbued with more enthusiasm than ever for the Army when he arrived at Gouverneur to spend that summer vacation. Highland Academy was so near West Point that he had been afforded a chance to view army life at first hand and had liked it.

According to Reverend John Lee Watson, a director at Highland, young Kearny became more interested in the doings at West Point than in his own studies. Some years later Watson wrote: "Philip ... came to our school ... with the intention of preparing himself for admission to Columbia College ... For a time he pursued his classical studies with great diligence, and gave much encouragement to his future progress ... But it soon became apparent that all his own inclinations tended toward a military education...."

To an impressionable youth West Point must have offered an exciting and glamorous panorama. Philip could hear the bugle calls from the other side of the Hudson; the drums and the sunset cannon echoed in the stillness of the valley. An observer had an unobstructed view of the Academy's parade ground from Highland's riverbank. Kearny bought a folding telescope, and at every opportunity was perched high in a tree on the shore, peering through his glass at the cadets at drill.

His enthusiasm for West Point was further whetted by those classmates preparing to take the Academy's entrance examination. And a lively traffic existed between West Point and Highland. An officer from the post came to Philip's school daily as a mathematics instructor; many officers stationed at the Academy had relatives attending Highland and often crossed the river to visit them. They all encouraged him to aim for West Point.

Among the frequent visitors were General Winfield Scott, the Commandant of West Point, and Colonel Sylvanus Thayer, the Academy Superintendent, known to history as the Father of West Point. Philip met them both at a tea given by Highland's headmaster. General Scott took an interest in the boy when he learned that his uncle was Major Stephen Kearny. Phil told the General of his wish to enter military service. Scott was pleased. "You may count on me for every assistance in helping you obtain an appointment to the Military Academy," he assured him.

The General's promise enflamed Philip. He made the definite decision that his goal was West Point and informed Reverend Watson. "I can no longer remain here under the guise of readying myself for entry into Columbia College," he explained. "I belong at West Point. The Army answers my dream for a life-long career." He asked Watson to change his curriculum so he could take the United States Military Academy's examination.

The reverend explained that this was not possible. "Your father enrolled you here for a specific purpose. I cannot disobey his wishes."

"Then I must leave Highland," young Kearny said.

Watson agreed that it would be dishonest for him to continue with his present course of study. "I respect your frankness in advising me of your feelings, Master Kearny, and shall tell your father and grandfather of this development when I send them my report of your progress here."

The school term ended and Philip shipped his personal belongings to Rose Hill and then journeyed to Gouverneur. For a week he spent the bright summer days riding and swimming. No one suspected the apprehension he felt while waiting for Watson's report to reach his father.

He was grooming a horse in the stableyard one morning when a servant told him his father wanted him in the library of the main house. The boy must have guessed the reason for the summons.

He found John Watts with Kearny, Senior. The latter addressed him in the exact tones he might have used before a company board of directors. He was "mortified, shocked and disgusted" by his son's "unsavory infatuation with the military" and warned him to "forget such nonsense."

"You will attend Columbia College in September and

study law. Upon graduation you will be taken into the office of my attorney, Peter Augustus Jay, and after a proper apprenticeship shall become an attorney. A lawyer will be invaluable to me in the brokerage business," the elder Kearny stated, as though pronouncing an ultimatum.

Philip tried to explain why he wanted West Point and the Army. He spoke of duty, patriotism, glory and love of country.

"Poppycock! Adolescent romanticism," his father sneered. "We live in a realistic world. You must learn to be a realist!"

When the desperate youth continued to plead his case the older man turned his back and stared out the window as though he heard nothing. This infuriated young Kearny. "I will not be a lawyer! You can't force me to do something I detest!" he cried.

The father swung around. "Mind your tone, sir! If you dare disobey me I'll turn you out with not a penny to your name. What will you do then—hawk newspapers?"

"I'll enlist as a private soldier!"

"Ridiculous! You are under age and I dare say I have influence enough to make any officer regret enrolling you." His father folded his hands. "This discussion is closed. I will not hear another word."

John Watts, who had been listening intently, broke his silence. "Wait! I have something to say. Philip, if you find the practice of law so distasteful it would please me should you study for the ministry." The old man went on to explain that since all his sons were dead he wanted his grandson to "wear the cloth." "Do this for me, my boy, and I will settle upon you an annual allowance of fifteen hundred dollars while you are studying and a much larger sum later."

"I'll not be bribed, Grandfather!" The boy was firm. Facing the two men, he continued. "I'm sorry to oppose your wishes, Father. And yours, Grandfather. But I have no desire for the law and no call for the ministry. I'm going to West Point. General Scott will help me, if you won't!"

"That's enough!" his father snapped. His open hand struck the boy's cheek in a humiliating blow.

Philip touched the spot where the blow had stung his skin. Gulping back tears, he fled from the room.

He ran across the broad lawn to the stables, brushing past a groom who was leading out a saddled horse for a waiting house guest. Phil vaulted onto the animal's back, yanked the reins from the startled groom, and galloped off. Hurdling a stone fence at full tilt, he sped down the long hill toward the village.

In 1830, Gouverneur was a stretch of green-shuttered, whitewashed frame houses along a hard-packed dirt road which also served as the village's main street. This was cut by a crossroad with one branch running west to the village of Natural Dam. The eastern arm passed through thick woods to Edwards. The north–south artery extended to Richville and Rensselaer Falls.

About a mile from Gouverneur, close to the bank of the Oswegatchie, smoke spiraled upward from the twin chimneys of a factory. Since the region abounded in limestone and soapstone deposits, a local plant had been established where the stone was ground into pumice and talc for commercial and industrial uses. The enterprise had not flourished and employed few villagers.

The surrounding countryside and all of St. Lawrence County was a noted dairy and agricultural center. Most of the inhabitants owned small, prosperous farms, although men such as Philip Kearny, Senior and John Watts controlled huge tracts.

On that hot August morning Gouverneur seemed deserted except for a few old men rocking on the shady porch of the general store. The houses were shuttered against the bright sunshine and the village dozed in the sultry morning. Even the farm dogs were satisfied to lie panting under the trees.

Young Kearny flashed by, raced his horse to the top of a long hill, then reined in so sharply that his mount reared. The boy leaped from the saddle and flung himself face downward in the fragrant grass.

His classmates at Highland and Round Hill had grown used to Philip's fits of anger. Usually he was good-humored and ebullient, but he pridefully refused to accept even the slightest defeat. If balked in any fashion he would give in to a swift rage that flared with the intensity of a brush fire in summer. These dark moods were only overcome by walking for miles or riding a horse at breakneck speed.

Sometimes in the throes of such passion he picked a fight. At Round Hill he had once instigated a free-for-all in the school dining room. One that ended with bloodied noses, blackened eyes, broken windows, smashed furniture and shattered crockery. Later Kearny wrote his cousin De Peyster: "We have had a Jim Dandy ruckus here; best described as a riot... worthy of Five Points or Paradise Square... I am ashamed to say it was I who started the melee by striking Benjamin Templeton... I had sufficient reason... But his friends took umbrage, some who supported my cause joined in... and bedlam broke out."

Although he was noted for his trigger temper, no one held a grudge against Philip, for once the storm had passed he was always ready to apologize. Schoolmates soon recognized the signs of a Kearny tantrum and stood clear until his fury spent itself.

Now, sprawled in the grass, he regretted the disrespect he had shown his grandfather. In later years he recalled: "I determined to make amends to Grandfather... For a moment I even considered promising him I would study for the ministry... But I could not abide hypocrisy...."

He realized that he must forget about West Point. "I never could have induced Father and Grandfather to give their consent... and since I had no independent means by which to subsist... I sadly accepted the reality that never would I have the honor of wearing cadet gray."

Because Phil Kearny was the product of a rigid stratum of society, it simply did not occur to him that he might have supported himself. In the United States at that time thousands of fifteen-year-old boys worked for a living. But Philip came from a background which precluded such a step. He was a gentleman's son and as such did not "labor for his daily bread."

Although a bad loser, Kearny never brooded long over a setback. He once said: "Even as a stripling I soon learned that a lost battle did not constitute total defeat... one could always fight again another day...."

Applying this philosophy he rode home, apologized to John Watts, and mollified his father by agreeing to study law at Columbia College.

In September he enrolled at Columbia as a sophomore. But with the help of his younger cousin John Watts De Peyster, who also lived at Rose Hill, kept alive his soldierly proclivities. Nearly all the leisure time of the two youths was taken up in conducting mock campaigns with armies composed of four to five thousand lead soldiers. According to De Peyster, "the troops were provided with artillery trains... and other adjuncts of a well-equipped host..."

Battles were fought under a set of rules which covered such details as "... the percentage of soldiers knocked down by musket or artillery fire that should be considered as dead or too severely wounded to take part in the rest of the campaign, and how many as slightly wounded, and how long the latter should be looked upon as remaining in hospital before they were again available."

The firing, done with small spring guns that hurled pellets, was governed by stringent regulations which permitted "one shot for each cannon, one for each regiment or separate detachment of infantry, and so many for each line of sharpshooters . . . Fieldworks and permanent fortifications were made of pasteboard and similar objects were built in accordance with agreement before operations commenced. One siege lasted a number of weeks . . . and the housekeeper . . . was driven nearly wild by the accumulation of dust and the appropriation of several huge mahogany tables whose oiling and polishing . . . were her pride and joy. . . ."

De Peyster also remembered that ". . . hostilities between the two generals would sometimes follow an argument, and the mimic warfare had to cease until the real conflict between the leaders was settled . . . often by fisticuffs. . . ."

It was during this period of mock warfare, which lasted from 1830 to 1834, that Kearny adopted the motto: *"Dulce et decorum est pro patria mori."* Through most of his college days he enjoyed the lead soldiers and their battles. But as De Peyster ruefully recalled: ". . . when Phil began to go about in society . . . he took much pains with his dress and spent so much time out of the house . . . that he gradually relinquished the game which had given him such delight and occupation for years . . ."

For Kearny, the make-believe warfare with the toy soldiers proved more than a pastime in later years. He used the game to work out intricate military maneuvers, strategy and tactics. His favorite gambit when playing with De Peyster was to launch a reckless cavalry charge. Invariably it failed and he rightly concluded that in real combat disciplined infantry could break a cavalry assault. However, more than a decade later he gained military fame by leading a vain and reckless cavalry charge. One day Kearny was to lose his partiality for cavalry and attain his highest rank as an infantry officer.

"The man who commands a cavalry regiment," he wrote, "has to perform a double duty ... He has to drill two regiments ... the one of bipeds, the other of quadrupeds, and I don't know but that the latter is easier to manage."

CHAPTER IV

KEARNY was a student at Columbia from September, 1830 until June, 1834. Though he lacked enthusiasm, he was a leading student. He had one of the natural endowments of a lawyer—a sharp, analytical mind. But he was too often ruled by impulse and emotion rather than by intellect. Throughout his life Philip never developed the ability to control the impetuousness which he too frequently responded when cool thinking was needed.

The years at Columbia were well spent. By the standards of his time Philip was looked upon as a highly educated young man with a solid background of Greek, Latin, mathematics, jurisprudence, history and literature.

But his feeling for the Army was as strong as ever; nothing could change that. If anything, his military ambitions were fanned at Columbia where his soldier uncle Stephen had been an undergraduate. Faculty members remembered the hero's student days and were proud of his feats in combat. Young Phil managed to keep his deepest feelings in abeyance and graduated with honors in June, 1834.

The four years at Columbia had developed him. He was no longer a boy but a handsome young man of nineteen with a commanding appearance.

He was preparing to go to Gouverneur for the summer as usual when Grandfather Watts intervened. The aged millionaire had a surprise for his grandson. As a graduation present Philip was to take the Grand Tour of Europe accompanied by John De Peyster.

Later Phil confided to his cousin that he had accepted the trip "with mingled emotions... I resented the autocratic manner with which *he* had decided what *I* was to do on my holiday. But the bait was too tempting... a prepaid European journey... I swallowed my pride for that."

"I was certainly relieved that Phil decided to go, since my journey hinged on his decision," De Peyster wrote a friend. "Knowing Phil, I was concerned that he might get stubborn and refuse the offer because no one had consulted him beforehand."

The boy had a marvellous summer. They lived well on the generous letter of credit which John Watts had given them in addition to buying round-trip passages for both. Phil's father had matched Watts' gift in money.

London, Paris, Vienna, Budapest and Rome awaited the travelers. De Peyster had drawn up a complex sight-seeing itinerary which Phil ignored. According to John: "... his only idea seemed to be looking at soldiers and their maneuvers ... He would be out of bed with the first dawn to wander forth and watch the exercises of a regiment of cavalry...."

"It was an elegant summer! A brilliant one," Kearny recorded in a letter.

BOOK TWO

1836–1847

"... glory is that bright tragic thing ..."

CHAPTER V

UPON his return from Europe, Philip clerked in the law office of Peter Augustus Jay. His days were spent with briefs and torts, writs and precedents. The sedentary occupation chafed him. Every morning he strode along Broadway from Rose Hill to Jay's office on William Street, far downtown. Smartly dressed, he moved with a long-legged cadence. De Peyster described him then as "a caged eagle or panther..." The daily hikes used up some of the energy that seethed within him.

No one knew that he was simply waiting until he became twenty-one when he intended to leave the law office and enter the Army. But this was two years away. "They were the most dismal years I have ever known," he said.

Attorney Jay was not happy with his unwilling charge,

either. "I believe young Kearny possesses high intelligence and a fine mind but lacks any interest in the legal profession," he noted in his journal.

The day came on June 1, 1836. Philip had intended to mark it by leaving his job on June 2 and applying for a commission in the Regular Army. But before he was able to do this John Watts suffered a sudden stroke that left him almost totally paralyzed. Phil could not bring himself to leave the helpless old man.

Watts lingered on until Saturday, September 3, 1836, when he died at the age of eighty-seven. His death gave young Kearny lifelong financial independence; his grandfather left him more than $1,000,000 in cash, property and investments.

Philip resigned from Jay's office and advised his father that he intended joining the Army. There was nothing Kearny, Senior could do; he no longer had any legal or financial hold over his son. One could not threaten an independent millionaire with the withdrawal of his allowance. His father reluctantly admitted defeat and the young man set out to get a commission.

At the time, the best regiment in the Army was the crack First United States Dragoons, commanded by Lieutenant Colonel Stephen Watts Kearny to whom his nephew applied for assistance. Philip also enlisted the aid of General Scott. With such backing he met with no obstacles at the War Department. On March 8, 1837, Secretary of War Joel R. Poinsett signed a second lieutenant's commission for Philip Kearny, Junior.

The newly appointed officer was assigned to the First

United States Dragoons, then stationed at Jefferson Barracks, Missouri. After making arrangements for the management and investment of his money Phil turned his back on a millionaire's life and set out on the arduous trip across country.

"Never had I been happier than the moment I began that journey," he wrote. "It was a pilgrimage to Mecca...."

He reported to his uncle on June 10, 1837, and served with the First Dragoons until May 21, 1839. Colonel Kearny did not believe in nepotism. He saw to it that the new lieutenant did line duty in the regiment's Company F which had been sent to the frontier and was based at bleak Fort Leavenworth, Kansas.

The unit safeguarded a vast territory against hostile Indians and remained constantly in the field. Lieutenant Kearny rode on long patrols, occasionally fought minor skirmishes with hostiles, and learned all the rigors of active service. He soon gained a reputation among the hard-boiled troopers as a "hunky-dory shoulder strap." In Army parlance of the day—a good officer.

Private Tom Elderkin, a soldier in Company F, wrote home:

The new shavetail, Kearny, is the Colonel's nephew but the boys like him all the same... He's a real high-class gentleman ... The boys think him a bit odd, though ... He's awful rich ... a millionaire, they say ... and the boys can't figure why anyone with all that money wants to be in the Army. Well, that's his business, I say ... Mr. Kearny does nice things ... if he sees a well-turned-out soldier with clean equipment and uniform ... why, he'll praise the man and give him a few bucks as a reward ... Does anything new turn up in saddles or equipment or the like . . . why, Kearny buys it out of his own pocket for us. . . ."

After more than a year of field service Philip was ordered back to Jefferson Barracks in August, 1838, and assigned as aide-de-camp to Brigadier General Henry Atkinson, the military district commandant. He stayed in that post until April 1, 1839.

At some point during this period he met Atkinson's sister-in-law, lovely Diana Bullitt, who had come from Louisville, Kentucky, to visit her sister at Jefferson Barracks.

Diana, a tall, brunette beauty, had many suitors but fell in love at once with dashing Lieutenant Kearny. He did indeed cut a romantic figure in his splendid dragoon uniform: gold-braided blue jacket with lace-trimmed collar and cuffs, blue-gray orange-striped trousers, plumed shako with silver and gold ornaments and gold foraging cords and tassels, orange sash and gleaming cordovan leather boots.

Kearny in turn was greatly attracted by Diana and spent all of his free time with her. They went horseback riding together and he was her constant partner at the officers' dances. Jefferson Barracks' gossip predicted an early wedding.

The General was pleased that his saucy sister-in-law seemed to have snared his wealthy aide; the General's wife reveled at the prospect of her younger sister marrying so well. But Philip did not propose. He had no desire to "... assume the responsibilities entailed in the wedded state ... There is much for me to do and I do not choose to trammel my opportunities for adventure ... by making a marriage now, no matter how delightful the prospective mate...."

At last Diana temporarily abandoned her campaign, but before going home she vowed to her sister: "I ... shall yet be Mrs. Philip Kearny."

They corresponded and Phil visited her in Louisville on a short leave. If outside events had not interfered he might have reconsidered his attitude about marrying. But an interesting military assignment intervened.

CHAPTER VI

AFTER the War of 1812 the United States Army had been drastically curtailed. Until 1833, it did not have a single cavalry regiment. That year the First Dragoons was activated, and because it was the only mounted troop, the Army lacked a suitable manual of cavalry tactics.

The Secretary of War became concerned about the situation. In 1839, he conceived the idea of sending to France three "promising dragoon officers" for the purpose of "... going through the regular course at the Royal School of Cavalry in Saumur ... and on their return ...the aforementioned officers would ... compile a work on cavalry tactics ... based on that of the French system, but so modified as to ... suit the wants of our service...."

At that time military experts regarded the French cavalry as the best in the world. President Van Buren endorsed places... nothing was wanting to make the affair a perfect success."

Kearny had to postpone the party several times. So many prominent persons requested invitations and he wished no one to be slighted. It was finally held on February 11, 1840. Philip's committee, with an unlimited budget, had stinted nothing. On entering the ball each lady was presented with a bouquet of flowers in an elegant silver holder. Each gentleman received a morocco leather-and-silver cigar case. An artist hired for the occasion made an oil painting of the ball while it was in progress; this was later presented to General Debrack as a souvenir.

Important military and civil dignitaries crowded the place. Ambassadors, princes, envoys, generals, businessmen and visitors from a dozen countries were present. According to one observer: "The fete was gotten up in a style of magnificence wholly unprecedented in that part of the country... It was a brilliant, coruscating affair... a spectacle not soon forgotten by any who witnessed it... There were striking uniforms; beautiful gowns... a sparkling agglomeration of colors, plumes, embroidery, lace and jewelry... sufficient to make one giddy with all the splendor..."

The party made Kearny the lion of French society. In fact, the affair delighted everyone but Kearny's financial agent in New York who "loosed a howl of anguish" when he totaled the amount that had been lavished on it.

"I believe young Kearny has lost his mind amidst those decadent Frenchies," the banker grumbled as he wrote a draft to cover the bill.

The result of these observations is intended to make known to our Government . . . the differences that exist in the organization, in the maneuvers . . . administrative, and all the internal regulations of the French cavalry and ours. Also, to inform us of the course pursued with the soldier from his joining as a recruit until admitted to the squadron . . ."

The Lucky Three were soon working diligently. Michaud, they agreed unanimously, was "a hard taskmaster" and the days at Saumur were busy ones. But there was time for fun as well, particularly during the Christmas season. On Twelfth Night (January 6, 1840) the Cavalry School Commandant, General Pierre Debrack, gave a party at his residence. It was a gala affair, for the French celebrated Twelfth Night with revelry.

Lieutenant Eustis recalled that Kearny ". . . was prevented by indisposition from attending the party . . . but the ladies sent him a piece of cake. This touched Phil and he said to me, 'I am going to hold a party to show my gratitude for the attentions these fine people have shown us.' "

Kearny's gesture mushroomed into the grandest social event Saumur had ever known. The huge main hall of the Cavalry School was made available for the fete. Phil turned over all the preparations to a group of French officers, giving them carte blanche as to expenditure.

Eustis wrote in his diary: "The hall was beautifully decorated under the personal supervision of General Debrack who was an artist of superior talents. The supper was sent from Paris by one of that city's most celebrated restaurateurs; flowers in profusion came from Angers and other

Saumur was situated on the left bank of the Loire River about 170 miles southwest of Paris. Kearny described it as "... a cheerful place, gleaming from afar with its white buildings ... a most picturesque town of quaint structures, towers, pinnacles and spires...."

The Royal School of Cavalry, which had been transferred to Saumur from Angers in 1768, was located in the southwestern sector of the city and consisted of spacious grounds, buildings, barracks and stables. Between three and four hundred officers and noncommissioned officers went there annually for instruction. After completing the course the graduates were distributed among the Army's various cavalry regiments, to train recruits.

Eustis, Turner and Kearny were assigned as pupils to Lieutenant Commander Michaud, a member of the faculty. In a report to Poinsett, Kearny described Michaud as "... an officer who stands high in his profession...."

Apparently Michaud had not been properly briefed on the status of his three American pupils, and Kearny clarified this for him in a letter:

My object—and that of my companions—is to remain at Saumur for six months or longer for the purpose of acquiring the French language, becoming instructed in the use of the sword and of arms pertaining to cavalry; to follow a course of riding, but rather the *practique* than the theory, and more especially for gaining ideas generally to assist us in more thoroughly visiting and making observations on the regiments themselves. Secondly, to visit some of the best dragoon and light-cavalry regiments; proposing also, should it be advisable and meet with the approval of our Secretary of War, to visit your regiments on active service in Africa.

Poinsett's idea and called on Colonel Stephen Kearny to choose three outstanding junior-grade officers for the mission. The men selected were First Lieutenants Henry Turner, William Eustis and recently promoted Philip Kearny.

On May 21, 1839, the three were relieved from "encumbering duties," put on detached service, and sent to Washington, D. C. ". . . there to report to the Secretary of War for further instructions . . ." On August 9 they were ordered to ". . . proceed to Saumur, France . . . for special duty."

"You can imagine with what joy I am undertaking this journey!" Philip exulted in a letter to John De Peyster.

The Lucky Three, as Army colleagues dubbed them, sailed from New York in mid-August. Philip had a brief reunion with his father, now reconciled to his son's profession, before sailing.

On October 1, 1839, the trio arrived at Fontainebleau where United States Ambassador Lewis Cass greeted them. King Louis Philippe was then in residence there and Mr. Cass presented the dragoons to him.

"His Majesty was most gracious," Kearny wrote an officer at Jefferson Barracks, ". . . and twice invited us to dine at the chateau . . . We remained several days at Fontainebleau at his request . . . and His Majesty generously permitted us to accompany his party . . . to a nearby camp of instruction where the troops staged a grand review. . . ."

On October 8, the American officers arrived at Saumur. Kearny had no inkling that his sojourn in France would be enlivened by an adventure to equal those of any of his dreams.

CHAPTER VII

DURING the latter part of 1839, trouble erupted in the French North African colony of Algeria. Reports from the scene suggested that a major Arab revolt was imminent. This occurrence was neither unusual nor unexpected. Warfare between Algerians and Frenchmen had flared sporadically since 1830, when France had wrested Algeria from Turkish rule and claimed the territory as her colony.

About 1836, Abd-El-Kader, an important sheik with vision and ideas, had risen to prominence as an anti-French leader. Abd-El-Kader's purpose was to unite all Arabs and establish an independent nation strong enough to drive out the French. At that time French holdings in Algeria were limited to the more densely populated areas along the seacoast: Algiers, Oran, Bougie and Bône, plus that territory immediately surrounding those cities.

All other parts of Algeria successfully resisted French encroachments. This was particularly true in the Constantine district. A French army had been routed there in 1836, but had come back the next year under Marshal Valée who subdued the region and set up an Arab puppet regime. Valée sought to negotiate a treaty with Abd-El-Kader, but the intransigent Arab leader refused to deal with the French. Instead he declared a holy war to recapture Constantine and annihilate the Foreign Legion, a mercenary force of adventurers from many lands which had been recruited by France to repress the Algerian natives. The Legion did its work ruthlessly with sword and fire. For Algerians the Legion epitomized French oppression.

Even as Kearny's ball was being held in Saumur, Abd-El-Kader's followers were ambushing Legion patrols and razing the French settlements in the hinterlands. Arab raiders swept to the very gates of Algiers, devastating the farms of French colonists adjacent to the city.

Marshal Valée called upon the national government for reinforcements, and a punitive expedition was mobilized for service against the insurgents. When Kearny heard that troops were being sent to Africa he sought permission from the War Ministry to join one of the regiments. Exploiting friendships he had made in military circles, he wangled an appointment to the staff of the duc d'Orléans as an honorary aide-de-camp, with a further assignment as a supernumerary officer in the First *Chasseurs d'Afrique*—the best cavalry regiment in the French Army.

All this pleased him, but Kearny could not accept these posts until given permission to do so by the United States

Secretary of War. Philip fretted and fumed at Saumur while waiting for word from Poinsett.

Eustis and Turner decided against seeking service in Africa and resolved instead to finish the course at Saumur, and afterward visit military establishments in England and on the Continent. Eustis sought to dissuade Kearny from the Algerian adventure. His diary read:

> I could see no point in Phil making the trip to Africa ... and facing unnecessary hazards. In vain I stressed that the purpose of our European mission was to gather data for a cavalry manual useful to the United States Army ... Since it was unlikely that our troops would ever engage in wholesale campaigns against Arabs ... I sought to convince Phil that his time could be more profitably spent elsewhere than in Algeria ... Turner agreed with my views ... but Phil remained adamant ... He said, "I don't care! I'm going ... I wouldn't miss this for a king's ransom ... If Poinsett does not grant the necessary permission I'll resign from the Army and join the Foreign Legion."

Such drastic action proved unnecessary. Although he received no direct word from Poinsett, Ambassador Cass told him that: "... the Secretary of War harbors no objections to your plan."

This was less than Kearny had hoped to hear, but good enough, although he complained to Poinsett in a letter:

> I recently mentioned ... that I thought it would be profitable to visit the regiments serving in Africa as there alone would I have the opportunity of observing troops in active service in the field ... You have not signified your opinion to me since receiving my communication ... but ... I presumed that had it not met your approbation ... you would have sig-

nified same to me. Indirectly and unofficially, however, I have heard that in respect to the plans in my letter, you made no objection; though, indeed, so unofficially has it reached me that I would not be justified in an ordinary case in considering it an authority...

While not wholly satisfied, Philip was at least sure that Poinsett did not mean to block him. With this assurance he made his arrangements. The duc d'Orléans reaffirmed Kearny's appointment as a staff officer and ordered him to Marseilles where the *Chasseurs* were waiting transport to Algeria. Then a few days before he was to quit Saumur for Marseilles, Kearny fell ill. He was helpless for weeks, and while incapacitated learned that the regiment had gone to Algeria and joined Valée in the field.

"Never have I been so disappointed and frustrated," Kearny wrote from his sickbed in Saumur. "I fear the campaign will end before I have recovered...."

Perhaps this illogical anxiety drove him to leave Saumur against his doctor's orders. No one could dissuade him from starting for Algeria on March 25, 1840, even though he was so weak that he had to be carried to his carriage on a litter.

Eustis was saddened by his departure. He confided in his journal: "... I would not be at all surprised ... if Phil leaves his bones in Africa...."

Only a month earlier at his grand party Kearny had radiated vigor and energy. Now he was thin and sunken cheeked but his eyes flashed defiance. His fighting spirit was aroused. No illness would defeat him. Since he could not go directly to Algeria in his present condition, Philip went to Paris where he remained under the care of a specialist who cured him in a month. By April 27, he was fit enough to board the packet boat that sailed weekly from Toulon.

On his arrival in Algiers Kearny hurried to Army Headquarters, only to find that the French Army was already fighting Abd-El-Kader. Under the circumstances he was not permitted to travel alone but would have to await a supply train which would be leaving in a week for Blida where Valée's troops were based.

Philip stalked angrily out of the Headquarters building, cursing the "bureaucrats and rear-echelon popinjays... who always hamstring a fighting man..." He probably would have gone into the desert to find the duc d'Orléans, but was dissuaded by some French officers who explained that the region between Algiers and Blida was swarming with Arab guerrillas. Kearny believed them when they described the tortures the Arabs inflicted on prisoners.

"Some practices of these desert nomads... were worse than those of our fiercest Indians... even the most bloodthirsty Comanche seemed mild mannered when compared to an Arab... At any rate my friends showed me that it would be madness to venture into the desert by myself," he recalled.

Traveling with the convoy for Blida, he reported to the duc d'Orléans on May 1. That nobleman, the King's eldest son, greeted the American warmly and introduced him to many high-ranking officers. The *duc*'s headquarters were located in a comfortable building, and for the next few days Kearny's only duties seemed to be attending splendid dinner parties as guest of honor.

This annoyed him. He had not traveled all the way to Africa for banquets. He complained to the *duc:* "For all the war I have seen, I may as well have remained in Paris."

The *duc* smiled. "Ah, my bold *ami,* you grow restless. Patience, Lieutenant, patience. I promise you shall soon have your fill of war and battle."

The duc d'Orléans kept his word. Within a week he summoned Kearny and handed him an envelope addressed to Colonel Le Pays de Bourjolly, commanding the First *Chasseurs d'Afrique.*

"This contains your orders for duty with the *Chasseurs,*" the *duc* said. "The regiment is encamped near Mount Mozaia, fifteen miles to the east. A supply column leaves within the hour. You may accompany it."

Kearny saluted, gathered up his gear, and an hour later was jogging across the desert on a sturdy cavalry horse. Battle-toughened mounted Foreign Legionnaires escorted the supply column. The weather was scorching, even for May in North Africa. The sun beat mercilessly on the slowly-moving convoy. Kearny pictured the glare of the sun on the sands "like the searing glow of ten thousand white-hot irons."

The terrain changed as the foothills of the Atlas Mountains were reached. The land became rugged and the mountain peaks that loomed ahead were snow capped. Mount Mozaia reared more than 5,000 feet high; a monstrous peak jutting above the rest like a gigantic fang.

The French Army's objective was Medeah, an Arab stronghold some ten miles away. A torturous and ancient road stretched between Blida and Medeah. It crossed Mount Mozaia through a defile called Tenyah Pass. Under ideal conditions it took seven hours of steady marching to traverse the mountain through the pass. A Danish military observer with the French Army described the region in a report to his government:

On both sides ... the defile is partially cultivated ... but the greater portion of the narrow path, slashed by many rivulets, leads through a rough thicket, sometimes interrupted by bold lime cliffs. Toward the crest of the range ... it becomes continually narrower; the cliffs from both sides approaching each other so closely that scarcely four men can march abreast; finally two conical rocks form a kind of natural gate ... In the depths below far to the right, so far down that its murmur can scarcely be heard ... roars an irresistible torrent which in dry season becomes a thread of water ... In the distance, through the pass soars the snow-capped peak of Mount Nador, beneath which nestles Medeah, bosomed in the luxuriant groves of fruit trees ...

The Dane concluded with the statement: "Marshall Valée has his work cut out ... fifty resolute men can hold Tenyah against a host..."

When Kearny joined the *Chasseurs d'Afrique* on May 8, at the base of Mount Mozaia, the regiment had made a fighting advance from Blida. Mounted Arab partisans had harassed the flanks and rear of the long French column all the way, and the *Chasseurs* had driven off a score of such attacks. "*Les Arabes* fought boldly, giving us shot for shot and cut of yataghan for slash of saber," commented a participant in these skirmishes.

Philip presented himself to Colonel Le Pays de Bourjolly

and was assigned to a troop. Only a few hours after his arrival he was in the saddle, helping to beat off a band of raiders who had ambushed a patrol. He displayed such coolness under fire that his company commander, the duc d'Aumale, Louis Philippe's youngest son, embraced him after the clash and cried, "My brave American! My gallant American! You have a French heart!"

In the next three days Kearny took part in many fights with the Arabs. Abd-El-Kader's men, he noted, "... rode like devils ... They hovered around a column all day until nightfall and from time to time charged upon us, shrieking their ululating war cry: 'Lu-Lu! Lu-Lu!' and brandishing their rifles ... When less than 100 yards away the marauders fired at us point blank ... The horses are trained to turn away of their own accord ... The rider then reloads and comes back to repeat his performance until killed or wounded..."

The *Chasseurs* improvised their own unorthodox tactics for combatting the Arabs. One would charge after the enemy, standing upright in the stirrups, "... sword in one hand, pistol in the other, the reins clenched in his teeth..." Kearny eagerly adopted this technique and even among the Arabs soon gained a reputation as one of the fiercest fighters in the *Chasseurs*.

"He was great in action, that Kearny," a former *Chasseur* recalled. "How many times I have seen him far in the advance, pursuing *les Arabes* ... sword and pistol ready ... the reins in his strong teeth ... He was *magnifique*, that Kearny ... A courtly, bold man, with the air of a *chevalier*, a knight ... But in battle his eyes glittered like an eagle's

... To him the smell of gunpowder and the whine of the bullets were as perfume and music..."

But Philip was not totally insensate to the horror of war. He wrote a New York friend:

I have seen and tasted combat in Africa. It is an abomination ... Brave and gallant men have died in agony around me... I have witnessed the mutilated bodies of our dead... I have seen men crazed by heat and thirst... Yet, unlike others, I am thrilled by the charge... It brings me an indescribable pleasure... I do not know why this is so... I love war... In it, I have found comradeship, devotion and brotherhood... More than ever I believe in my motto: *dulce et decorum est pro patria mori*. Every man must some day face death... I pray mine will come in the swirl of the fray...

The duc d'Orléans joined the Army at Mount Mozaia on May 11, and at 3 A.M. on May 12, ordered his shock troops drawn up for an attack on the formidable heights. The *duc* pointed to the mountain crest and the entrenchments which crowned it. In the bright moonlight the soldiers could see the Arabs moving about on the slope.

"*Mes enfants*," the *duc* cried, "the enemy is expecting us, and France is looking on!" He drew his sword with a flourish and shouted, "For France! *En avant!*"

The troops loosed a roaring cheer and rushed toward the mountain. In a moment the scarped flank of the rocky heights was covered with yelling soldiers. They leaped, climbed and scrambled up the steep slope. Officers urged on their men. Despite Arab resistance, the French pressed ahead. The attackers suffered many casualties. Abd-El-Kader's men delivered a murderous fire from behind the cover of the rocks and well-placed breastworks. The crackle of musketry became continuous.

Soon thick gun smoke enveloped the mountain like a cloud, and the anxious men waiting below could not see what was happening farther up the mountainside. Until after dawn no news came to Marshal Valée and the duc d'Orléans. At last couriers and walking wounded brought back word that the troops on the mountain needed reinforcements. The duc d'Orléans did not hesitate. He ordered the *Chasseurs* dismounted, and at the head of the regiment led it into the battle.

Kearny was in the midst of that fighting. He organized a bayonet charge which dislodged a stubborn pocket of Arab resistance. The battle moved slowly toward the mountain peak as Abd-El-Kader sullenly retreated, yielding ground a foot at a time. At 3 P.M., after twelve hours of steady combat, the *tricolore* was finally planted on the mountain peak and the Arabs fled helter-skelter down the reverse slope. Tenyah Pass had been taken.

Kearny remained with the *Chasseurs* until Medeah was captured in mid-June after a hard siege. By then the heat had grown so intense that no further fighting could be undertaken. He had participated in many battles and absorbed an important and vital military lesson—the value of well-trained infantry. "I can never sufficiently praise the valor, determination and discipline of the French infantryman," he said. "Cavalry such as the *Chasseurs* can be an asset, but an army survives or perishes on the strength of its foot soldiers. . . ."

In Algeria, Philip learned soldiering as few graduates

of military academies could have. He won the respect of the *Chasseurs* who labeled him Kearny *le Magnifique*.

By the time Medeah was captured they had lost so many horses from wounds, heat and exhaustion that the regiment had to fight on foot, although mounts were still available for officers. Philip refused a horse and marched in the ranks. He never fell out, no matter how grueling the route, encouraged those near him, and helped any who weakened. "More than once Kearny came into bivouac carrying two or three muskets and as many knapsacks for weary soldiers," a veteran remembered.

On July 15, he bade farewell to his comrades and returned to France—a lean, wiry, sunburned soldier. The ribbon of the cross of the Légion d'honneur made a splash of color on his tunic. The duc d'Orléans had pinned it there for "... services to France ... above the call of duty...."

CHAPTER VIII

IN SEPTEMBER, 1840, Philip Kearny stood at the rail of a passenger ship moving slowly up New York Harbor. He had been away more than a year and was returning with mixed feelings. "I regretted leaving France, and yet yearned for my native land . . . and familiar faces."

His mission had been successful. Poinsett had written a glowing letter in which he assured him that: "your future in the Army is bright . . ."

He was not so confident. The peacetime American Army seemed a tame prospect after fighting in Algeria. Promotions came slowly in the American Army. Actually, a few days before sailing he had made a difficult choice. The duc d'Orléans, about to organize a new Foreign Legion regiment, had offered him the post of regimental executive officer with a lieutenant colonel's rank if he would volunteer for the Legion.

"You shall have combat, glory and adventure!" the nobleman had declared. "Think of it, *mon ami*, a lieutenant colonel at twenty-five!"

He had thought hard. In the United States Army he would have to wait ten years—even longer—before reaching that rank. The prospect of action with the Legion had been tempting. He liked the French way of life; the customs of the country and the temperament of the people suited him. But Kearny could not bring himself to resign from the army of his own country.

"What am I, if not an American?" he had asked a group of Legion officers who urged him to accept. "My duty is to serve under the Stars and Stripes, not the *Tricolore*. The Legion is for men who have either forsaken their own countries or have been forsaken by them. No! As much as I love France, I love the United States even more."

At Rose Hill Philip had a melancholy reunion with his father. The older man was ailing. He had changed drastically during the year of his son's absence; he was shrunken and wrinkled, with clouded, almost vacant, eyes. Most shocking to Kearny, his father's clothes were rumpled and untidy. For one who had always prided himself on his stylish dress he was now utterly indifferent to his slovenly appearance.

"I feel pity for Father," Phil wrote his uncle at Jefferson Barracks. "Seeing him thus brought to mind a great oak which once stood near our house in Gouverneur. It had been there like a leafy giant for decades, but one summer it began to die. Slowly... miserably; eaten by an invisible blight, until near summer's end naught but its rotted shell remained. Father is like that splendid tree; he is no longer a man, but a moldering hulk."

Kearny had been given an indefinite leave to remain with his father, but only two weeks after his return Kearny, Senior died during the night, spared the indignity of long suffering from his malignant disease.

"Unfortunately, only in the waning days of Father's life did we effect a rapport; during those last few weeks there was a bond between us for the first time in my memory," Kearny reflected, in writing his uncle.

On his father's death Philip inherited a second fortune. Despite this increased wealth he chose to remain in the Army and applied for active service with his old regiment, the First Dragoons. But Secretary Poinsett had different employment to offer him: the most coveted post in the Army—that of aide-de-camp to Major General Alexander Macomb, the Commander in Chief.

Kearny protested the appointment vigorously and demanded line duty where his Algerian experience would be of value, but Poinsett held firm and in early November, 1840, Phil reported to Macomb at Washington.

He soon came to detest the protocol and punctilio that went with a job in which the duties were chiefly social.

After several unhappy months his stay in the National Capital was unexpectedly brightened by the presence of Diana Bullitt. Lovely "Die," a descendant of the Revolutionary War hero, George Rogers Clark and of Captain William Clark, co-leader of the Lewis and Clark expedition, possessed all the tenacity of her famous forbears. She renewed her efforts to capture Kearny and this time was successful.

He proposed in April, 1841, and on June 24, the pair was married at what Washington called: "...the most opulent [affair] ever held in the Capital."

The sudden death of General Macomb on the following day canceled the couple's plans for a New York honeymoon. Philip was kept busy with administrative detail, and it was not until the beginning of August that he and Diana arrived in Manhattan. They spent several weeks in a round of soirees, fetes and galas. Though it was summer, New York society was eager to please young Kearny.

A society reporter on the New York *Herald* wrote: "... this summer has seen more parties than in many years past... Garden teas, outdoor entertainments, dinners alfresco and galas have enlivened the social world... and all this activity to honor Lieutenant Philip Kearny and his beauteous bride...."

Philip took his wife to Gouverneur and they held a reception in the old house. "It was...a spectacle...of wealth, elegance and splendor...." an observer reported.

The Kearnys returned to Washington in mid-October. Again he tried to obtain a field assignment, but instead was given a post at the War Department. He hid his chagrin and "gallantly fought the battle of paper...I shuffled papers, papers, papers...I could not help feel that if that immense paper pile ever dropped on me I would be buried ... as if trapped in an avalanche...."

Washington became "that heavenly place" to Diana. She was delighted with the teas, embassy receptions, formal dinners and balls which marked fall and winter in the Capital.

Philip bought a townhouse in the city's most fashionable district, and Diana's days were occupied with decorators, upholsterers and painters.

For a short time Kearny was ordered to the United States Cavalry Barracks at Carlisle, Pennsylvania, where he once again met Eustis and Turner. The reunited Lucky Three had been called there to prepare a proper cavalry manual based on their observations at Saumur, in other countries, and Kearny's Algerian experience.

This assignment lasted until early December, 1841, and the Kearnys spent Christmas in Washington. Diana had the house ready, a feat she had accomplished only through prodigious effort and expense. The housewarming was a Christmas Day reception. Soon this home became the hub of the Capital's social life. Kearny was pleased; Diana proved to be a splendid hostess as well as a good companion. His delight increased when she told him that they were going to have a child.

He would have been completely happy except for the progress of his career. His next post did not suit him either. The brilliant but arrogant Winfield Scott was promoted to Major General and appointed to succeed Macomb. The new Commander in Chief, given to elaborate uniforms and martial pomp, was known in army circles as

Old Fuss and Feathers. Scott selected the most dashing young officers he could find for his staff; as aide-de-camp he chose Philip Kearny.

In General Scott, Kearny found a man whose temperament matched his own. The General was fearless and iron willed; haughty and proud. He was strikingly handsome, and in dress uniform dominated any group of which he was part. Old Fuss and Feathers, like Phil, was quick to anger and as quick to relent.

An astute observer once remarked: "Seldom have I known two men so much alike as General Scott and his aide, Lieutenant Kearny... In taste, temperament and talent this pair has been similarly endowed through some quirk of nature... They are as father and son... Kearny may easily project himself into the future... for he is a reflection of the General... He will be tomorrow as General Scott is today...."

CHAPTER IX

KEARNY served as Scott's aide from December, 1841, until April, 1844. "It grows increasingly apparent to me that my function is not that of a soldier, but rather as the dispenser of elegant hospitality...." he wrote De Peyster after many months of this duty.

This unflattering but accurate statement summed up his role. During the winter social season a night seldom passed without Scott giving some kind of party.

The General's most important social affairs were often held in the Kearny mansion, since Scott's house was not suitable for large gatherings. Diana Kearny was a skillful hostess for the General. Statesmen, soldiers and diplomats were charmed by her. "Everyone in Washington adored Die

... she was a flower, a poem, a song of rapturous beauty..." an admirer commented.

If Diana was Washington's favorite, her husband became her counterpart. Kearny had every attribute necessary to a general's aide-de-camp. No one of any consequence in Washington ever gave a party without inviting the Kearnys.

But as time passed Phil grew ever more irritable and unhappy. He bickered and quarreled with fellow officers. Too often he had to saddle a fast horse and ride off a burst of anger. Not even Diana was spared his savage moods; the great hall of the Kearny home often rang with his outbursts as he subjected her to his frustrations.

Only when the baby was born in June, 1842, did Philip's behavior modify. He cherished the infant daughter who had been named Susan after his mother. On sunny afternoons he left the General's office and hurried home to take Susan for her airing. Passers-by smiled at the dragoon officer wheeling a baby carriage at march step, his saber clanking, while behind him trotted a plump nursemaid.

But in January little Susan became ill and died at the age of nine months. Kearny was desolate. For weeks he neglected his duty and was short with everyone including General Scott. The General did not reprimand him; he understood Philip's grief and sympathized.

For awhile Diana suffered the most from Kearny's behavior; he was surly and indifferent to her. Not only had she lost her child, but apparently her husband as well.

At last Philip emerged from the grip of his sullen melancholia. He again treated his wife with tender consideration, and a closer relationship developed between them, as though their loss had created a depth of understanding which had been lacking before.

The Kearny house once more became the center of Washington gaiety. Philip resumed his duties with energy and spirit and appeared everywhere at Scott's side, the trim, efficient aide.

In May, 1843, Kearny heard with joy that he was to become a father for the second time. Yet even this welcome news began to pall. His contentment had merely been on the surface; the stifling dissatisfaction of his position as the General's aide still festered.

"Am I to spend my military career as a highly placed flunky looking to floral decorations in banquet rooms, escorting visiting bores, and dancing with the ugly wives and clumsy daughters of foreign diplomats? Am I to remain the obsequious major-domo of the Commandant's retinue?" he asked in a letter to a New York friend.

Once again he rode an emotional toboggan into another valley of depression. Not even the birth of a second daughter—Diana—on January 4, 1844, entirely dispelled his gloom.

His relations with Scott deteriorated. On several occasions Kearny's behavior toward the General almost approached insubordination. However, Scott was patient. He had a genuine affection for Philip in whom he saw: "... tremendous potential as a military leader ... if ever a man were a born soldier he is Phil Kearny ... He has been endowed with ardor and courage ... Soldiers will follow such a man to the very gates of Hell."

But eventually Kearny went too far. One day early in

April, 1844, Scott asked him to arrange a dinner for a European military mission. He raised a mild objection to the seating arrangement Phil suggested. Kearny became livid with anger and an observer later alleged that he had shouted: "Sir, I am a soldier, not a butler!"

The General gasped. "How is that, sir? You dare address me in such terms?"

"If you do not like the seating plan do it yourself!"

"Not another word, Mr. Kearny! Not a whisper!" the General bellowed. "Another sound and I'll have you court-martialed."

Philip managed to control his temper and left the room. Later Scott reprimanded him severely and Kearny apologized, but both agreed that it was time for Phil to take another assignment.

Before the month had ended, orders came relieving him from duty on Scott's staff and sending him to the First Dragoons at Fort Leavenworth, Kansas.

Kearny was satisfied. He would be with his old outfit—men he looked upon as "real soldiers, not pompous pencil-pushers..." At Fort Leavenworth there was a possibility of action against hostile Indians. "I find this change of station most gratifying," he wrote De Peyster.

But Diana found the prospect appalling. She could not journey to Kansas with a four-months-old infant, and while officers' families did reside at the post it was scarcely a place to raise a child. Life in a frontier garrison did not appeal to her. She had experienced it when visiting her sister and General Atkinson. Besides, she liked her position as Washington's leading young hostess and was reluctant to give it up.

Diana told all this to Kearny and they decided that she and the baby should remain in Washington until his tour of duty out West was completed. This separation was the first open indication that their marriage had failed.

CHAPTER X

KEARNY left Washington on May 1, 1844, and reached Fort Leavenworth eleven days later. He was glad to see many old friends including Eustis and Turner. His uncle, now a full colonel, put him in command of Company F—the most troublesome unit in the regiment.

In many companies of the First Dragoons the desertion rate was high. There were fights, insubordination and disorder. This did not hold for Company F after Kearny took over; he worked the men hard and kept them to a rigid training schedule. His regimen produced gripes and grumbles. A few troopers vowed to "... to get the dude shoulder stripe..." Yet even the worst ruffian in Company F had to admit that Kearny was a good officer, for if he worked his men hard, no one worked harder than he. In Africa he had learned the most important aspect of leadership, which he described as "... never to order a private soldier to do that which I would not do myself...."

Philip remembered this precept and always led his company by example. No soldier in Company F was a more daring rider, a better shot, or a finer swordsman. At times he treated his soldiers severely, giving them no more than regulations allowed, yet he always dealt fairly and justly with them.

He looked after his men. In a short time the whole regiment admitted that Company F troopers were eating better than the rest. Kearny showed solicitude to the sick and the injured, but cracked down hard on troublemakers, malingerers, sneak thieves and cheats.

"No man I command will disgrace with impunity flag, country, uniform, regiment or company. I shall punish offenders to the hilt," he warned.

This admonishment had results. Kearny's command had the lowest courts-martial record in the First Dragoons. To his dismay the frontier remained completely tranquil. The Indian tribes were all at peace and the regiment had little to do. He found that duty at Leavenworth was no more exciting than it had been in Washington and far less comfortable.

The days were spent drilling, parading and training. Every month the officers were hosts at a dance for the garrison's ladies. These drab affairs bored Philip. At night, after duty hours, most officers either gambled or got drunk.

Whisky did not appeal to Kearny and he detested cards. He found Fort Leavenworth a deadening place and grew to hate it.

After a year in this atmosphere a growing disenchantment with the Army overwhelmed Kearny. He had been a soldier almost ten years, and but for the interlude with the French in Algeria, was forced to admit ". . . I have experienced no more adventure than that which might befall a ribbon clerk in a New York City emporium."

He was free to resign his commission whenever he chose, yet he stayed on. Perhaps he did so in the hope that the boredom and monotony would soon end. Any day could bring action and glory. Perhaps pride kept him from quitting—Kearny seldom admitted to a mistake. Perhaps he remained because of the growing awareness that his marriage was foundering.

In a year he exchanged little communication with Diana. Once he had journeyed to Washington on leave in November, 1844, and subsequently received word that another baby was expected in July. Despite this, the rift between them was widening. By remaining a soldier on the frontier Kearny did not have to face that unpleasant development squarely.

In May, 1845, the regiment was ordered on a mission that Philip believed would bring the action he craved. Five dragoon companies under Colonel Stephen Kearny made a reconnaissance in force through the heart of the Indian Territory to the foothills of the Rocky Mountains.

The reason for this long march was to awe the Sioux and other warlike tribes with a display of military power. Even more important, the troopers would be in a position to protect the immigrant wagon trains rolling along the Oregon Trace in growing numbers. This was the first large Army expedition ever to penetrate those regions. The troops were equipped to stay in the field for several months.

The line of march led the dragoons through a country abounding in game and buffalo—the richest of Indian hunting grounds. Each day the soldiers pushed farther into Indian territory, but no hostiles challenged them.

According to Kearny, the reconnaissance proved to be "... a pleasant junket... We marched to Fort Laramie, thence through South Pass and returned via Laramie to Bent's Fort near Pikes Peak, southward to the Santa Fe Trail, and thence north to Fort Leavenworth... we covered 2,300 miles in 99 days and lost not a single man through accident or illness, and but a few horses... The only Indians we saw at close hand were some Sioux chieftains with whom Colonel Kearny held council and exacted from them the promise that travelers on the Oregon Trace would not be molested..."

The expedition was hailed as a success, and a grateful War Department—which had anticipated Indian uprisings because of the traffic to Oregon—brevetted Colonel Kearny to the rank of brigadier general. Everyone but Phil was pleased by the march; he was deeply disappointed. There had been no action; no deeds of valor had been performed. He sulked in his quarters at Fort Leavenworth and again sank into somber moods. Not even the news that Diana had given birth to a son on July 25 raised his spirits. She had gone home to Paducah, Kentucky, and was with her family when the baby came. The new arrival was named John Watts, thus breaking the Kearny tradition of christening the first son Philip.

In October, 1845, Philip took an extended six-months leave. He brought Diana and the children from Paducah to Rose Hill and spent the long winter pondering his future. These deliberations ended in his resignation from the Army.

He promptly set about making a permanent life for himself and his family in New York City, selling the Washington mansion and having their furniture there shipped to New York.

Diana wrote her sister: "Perhaps... at long last, after these past stormy years... Phil and I may yet find some peace...."

Kearny's retirement became official on April 2, 1846. That day his wife confided to a friend: "I feel as though an oppressive weight has been lifted from me... I have won back my husband."

Her triumph was short lived. Events in Texas soon shattered her optimism. For months unrest had been rising along the Rio Grande River. Rumors of an impending war with Mexico grew daily. The ferment had brewed ever since Texas had gained independence from Mexico ten years before.

With the granting of statehood to Texas—the Lone Star Republic—by the United States in December, 1845, the situation had become critical. The Mexicans looked upon the admission of Texas to the Union as a belligerent act by the United States. Both countries rushed troops to the border and hostilities began on April 23, 1846.

Only a few days after his resignation had gone into effect Kearny saw that he had been wrong to leave the Army. The country was at war and he wanted to be in the thick of it. Ignoring Diana's tearful pleadings, he sped to Washington and sought to have his resignation withdrawn. General Scott helped him gain reinstatement; even better, Old Fuss and Feathers gained a promotion to captain for Kearny with rank dating from April 15, 1846.

Diana was crushed by her husband's actions. "I believe that it matters not to Phil whether I am in New York, return to Paducah, or live among the Hottentots. He cares only for the Army and to participate in the war . . . I am at a loss . . . Perhaps I shall stay here awhile . . . I am well provided for materially . . . The children and I want for nothing except the love of father and husband. . . ." the unhappy woman wrote her sister.

Kearny remained unmoved by his wife's distress. His only response was an increase in her already liberal allowance. He was "gloriously overjoyed" that a real war was at hand—one he could fight under his own flag. "The time has come from prodigous feats of courage and honor. I shall not fail the moment!" Philip wrote a friend.

"Wife, children, home ties, were merely leaden weights

hobbling Kearney, the warrior, whose eagle spirit now soared unfettered. He was free at last, torn loose from the mundane world where men lived drab lives without adventure and peril," observed Cortland Parker, Kearney's attorney.

CHAPTER XI

THE first wartime order Philip received was to again take command of Company F, First United States Dragoons. However, by the outbreak of the Mexican War that unit existed only on paper; the enlistment terms of most of the men in the company had expired. Kearney's mission was to recruit the company up to authorized combat strength—120 men. He determined to make it a model company in every respect—not only with the caliber of the men he would muster, but also the quality of the horses they were to ride and their equipment in general.

He decided that both men and mounts could most easily be found in the West, and traveled to Springfield, Illinois, where he established a recruiting headquarters. Philip issued a call for "... dauntless patriots who excel in horsemanship and the use of firearms..." As an inducement he offered to match the $100 government-enlistment bounty out of his own pocket. In addition he bought his men the finest saddles, weapons and personal outfits to be found.

Most important to him was his selection of horses. A Springfield lawyer—a tall, gangling man named Abraham Lincoln—helped Phil find the proper mounts by introducing him to the best horse breeders in the region.

By early July, Company F was fully manned, armed and equipped. Kearny received orders to join the rest of the regiment on the Texas border. The troop passed through New Orleans en route and the appearance of Company F caused a stir in the Crescent City. The New Orleans *Tropic* ran a long article on Kearny's command, stating in part: "... Captain Philip Kearny, nephew of Stephen Watts Kearny, arrived here with ... as fine a company of cavalry as was ever seen in New Orleans ... The horses, one hundred and twenty in number, are matched grays and truly beautiful specimens ... The dragoons are picked and noble-looking fellows ... The trappings of the horses ... and riders are all that a fastidious commander could wish ... They will doubtless give a good account of themselves on the field of battle."

Irksome delays on the way held up Company F so that it did not meet the First Dragoons until October 1, 1846, when the regiment was at Camargo, Mexico. Kearny's troopers spent a few uneventful weeks scouting and patrolling in that area. He employed the plentiful spare time in a rigorous training of them for coming hardships. He drilled his dragoons until, according to observers, the company was "a masterpiece of military excellence...."

During the last week of October the regiment, including Company F, marched to the front near Saltillo, Mexico, to serve under General Zachary Taylor. Old Rough and Ready had pushed on to Saltillo after capturing Monterrey. But by the time the First Dragoons came onto the scene the fighting in the Monterrey-Saltillo sector had ended and only routine duties were left for the regiment to perform. That condition did not last long. Late in November, General Scott completed plans to seize Vera Cruz and drive northward to Mexico City from there.

To reinforce this operation Scott stripped Taylor of several regiments which were marched to the Coast and put aboard ship for transport to Vera Cruz. Scott's initial order to Taylor concerning the transfer of troops carried the following instructions: "... you will immediately put in movement for the mouth of the Rio Grande ... 500 regular cavalry of the 1st and 2nd Dragoons including Kearny's troop...."

Before long, Scott landed his forces near Vera Cruz and that important center came under siege. Toward the close of December, Old Fuss and Feathers reviewed the troops under his command. He was so impressed by the splendid condition of Kearny's unit that he made Company F his personal bodyguard.

Thus Philip once again found himself at a headquarters' post. Company F did not take active part in the frequent skirmishes between United States Dragoons and Mexican Cavalry, but Phil did not regret missing those fights. Proximity to Scott gave him an excellent opportunity to gain first-hand experience in dealing with command problems.

The siege of Vera Cruz lasted until the end of March, 1847. When the city finally capitulated, Kearny's company escorted General Scott on his triumphal entry into the town. Even the Mexicans applauded the appearance of the bodyguard. According to Phil, the men were proud of the place of honor they held. He wrote Cortland Parker: "The boys were up most of the previous night... furbishing their arms and accoutrements... and grooming the horses ... so their coats shone like glass bottles in the morning sunlight..."

After Vera Cruz fell, General Scott advanced on Mexico City. While Kearny's dragoons took little part in the fighting along the way, he absorbed much valuable information about strategy and the handling of large bodies of troops by watching Scott in action.

On April 18, Company F had its chance to see combat during the Battle of Cerro Gordo. All at once the Mexicans, who had been resisting bravely, panicked and fled in a total rout toward Mexico City. Scott decided to pursue, and Company F was the only mounted unit available.

"Kearny, ride after the enemy! Smash him! Take prisoners! If possible bring in General Santa Anna," Scott ordered.

Within minutes Company F was galloping after the routed enemy. Kearny rode like a true *Chasseur,* pistol in left hand, saber in right, teeth clamped on the reins. Infantrymen gawked as he thundered by; they had never seen this desert-style charge. An awed New York volunteer wrote home: "He was a fearsome sight, that dragoon captain, as he came riding like the devil was after him..."

Kearny's "boys" failed to capture General Santa Anna, but did cause confusion in the Mexican ranks. The dragoons hacked and slashed until darkness came; the Mexicans kept up their fight beyond Puebla. At that city Scott ordered a halt for "rest, regrouping, replacements and replenishment..."

A lull fell over the fighting front, but the idle time did not hang heavily on Kearny. He was entrusted by General Scott with several important reconnaissances, and Company F guarded a topographical and survey team of engineers who mapped out the route to Mexico City. Commanding the engineers was a Virginian, Colonel Robert E. Lee. Since the enemy avoided giving battle, Philip "gained no laurels."

During the stay at Puebla a group of officers from Scott's staff were tendered a dinner by Kearny. The guests discussed the forthcoming attack on Mexico City and unanimously agreed that the enemy would defend his capital with "desperate fury."

"Yes, there will be hot fighting," Philip agreed. "Fighting and glory for all. That pleases me. I want to win glory in combat. I would give my left arm for a brevet to major and the acclaim of my countrymen!"

Shortly after the Puebla dinner Scott resumed the forward movement. The Americans drove the enemy to the gates of the Capital in a series of battles. By Friday, August

20, 1847, Scott's 9,000 men were at the fortified village of Churubusco on the outskirts of Mexico City.

A staff officer described the situation:

> In front of Scott... occupying the village of Churubusco... and in a chain of well-constructed strong points were some 30,000 Mexican troops... backed by the population of Mexico City... which could turn out, if they so willed, 50,000 males capable of bearing arms... The Mexican forces, outnumbering ours three or four to one, held the village which is... of solid construction... Along their line of battle were hedges of thorny maguey or cactus behind which lurked snipers and sharpshooters... Enemy fieldpieces swept the roadway... The land was broken and difficult, criss-crossed by enclosures, morasses, canals, and ditches... in addition, the Mexicans had dug an interlacing network of trenches...

This was Churubusco. The village had strategic importance because it straddled the junction of several good roads which led to Mexico City. The Via San Antonio, the principal highway, bisected the village and continued due north for five and one-half miles, terminating in the Grand Plaza of Mexico City.

The Via crossed the Churubusco River over a stone bridge which was strongly guarded by an artillery battery of the *San Patricio* Battalion, a unit made up of Irishmen who had deserted the American Army and gone over to the Mexican side.

These *San Patricios*—some 250 men—had vowed to make a finish fight; each knew he could be executed for desertion if captured. In addition to the battery the bridge was guarded by scores of Mexican riflemen.

General Scott had the Mexican positions carefully scouted. The reports his patrols brought back were discouraging. The enemy had thrown up defensive works described as "admirable both in their construction and location..." The bridgehead or *tête-de-pont* was especially well built. It was protected by abatis, embrasures, fascines and cleverly placed guns. About 250 yards southwest of this bastion rose the massive Convent of San Mateo, a stone building centuries old. The convent and its garden, around which ran a thick stone wall, had been converted into a fortress.

Squads of infantry defended the convent, the out buildings and the garden. High up in the convent tower the guns of sharpshooters bristled. At the *tête-de-pont* the banks of the Churubusco River rose higher than the surrounding tableland across which the Americans had to attack. The northern bank, from the convent to the bridge, swarmed with Mexican infantry; and for a thousand yards in the direction of Mexico City the Via San Antonio was lined with rank upon rank of infantry and cavalry waiting in reserve. General Santa Anna had risked all of his troops in a gamble to hold Churubusco; here the fate of Mexico City was to be decided.

Kearny felt that the coming battle might prove to be the most crucial of the war. He did not relish sitting out the struggle in Scott's headquarters, and requested that Company F be relieved of its assignment as the General's bodyguard. Scott understood Kearny's desire to take part in the fighting and released the dragoons for full duty with General Floyd Pillow's division. Kearny's command was attached to the cavalry brigade under Colonel W. S. Harney.

All that Friday morning the Americans and Mexicans skirmished near Churubusco, but it was noon before Scott launched his main attack. Under the hot Mexican sun the Americans moved out to storm the village.

"The enemy fought as he never had before," an American officer declared. "The roar of Mexican musketry was the greatest noise of all the battle din; it was continuous and terrific, drowning the crash of artillery, the shouts of the combatants, the shrieks of disemboweled horses and the ghastly cries of wounded men...."

The primary objective of Scott's assaulting force was to take the bridgehead. The attackers ran into determined resistance. "Death to the gringos!" the defenders shouted as they pounded the oncoming Americans with shot and shell.

The advantage lay with the defense. The attacking troops were forced to wallow across a twenty-foot moat filled with muddy water nearly four feet deep. The charging Americans stumbled on the rough ground; whole companies became entangled in its thorny thickets. American cannon mired down on the boggy riverbank and every approach to the *tête-de-pont* was swept by Mexican grapeshot.

The fire from the convent smashed the American ranks again and again until the ground was covered with dead and wounded. Despite awful losses, Scott pressed the attack. The battle roared on for more than three hours in the grueling August heat. At last American infantry crossed the Churubusco far to the right of the battle line and turned the Mexican left flank, making the enemy positions at both bridgehead and convent untenable.

General Santa Anna tried to draw back his troops in an orderly manner, but dismay spread among the Mexicans. Conflicting commands confused the men, and while some units retreated, others held their ground, especially at the bridgehead and the Convent of San Mateo. The Americans had to launch a bayonet attack against those strong points. The attack was successful, but the *San Patricios* did not surrender until only 49 men remained of the battalion's original 250.

As the bitter fight for the bridgehead and convent reached its peak Kearny was with Pillow, who had captured Coyacán, a tiny village on the Churubusco River some miles to the east. Once again Kearny fretted that he would be "cheated out of the action." Pillow had entered Coyacán without meeting any resistance. The only obstacles hindering the Americans were the ditches and thickets of the marshy terrain. The rough ground bothered the dragoons, who feared their horses might fall in the unsure footing.

From Coyacán, Company F pushed across country to within a mile of the Via San Antonio where Kearny was joined by Company K, Third Dragoons, under Captain A. T. McReynolds. At that time the battle for the bridgehead and convent had not yet been decided and Pillow hoped to turn the Mexican flank by hurling his dragoons against the enemy.

With McReynolds following, Phil led the attempt. The maneuver failed. "The ... wide and marshy fields ... served as an effective barrier that ... prevented us from reaching the enemy's lines ... our horses sank to the withers in mud...." Kearny remembered.

After abandoning the flanking movement the dragoons returned to their positions near the Via San Antonio and awaited orders. At about 4 P.M. a courier brought General Pillow word that the bridgehead had fallen, along with the convent. Soon the Mexican Army came up the Via in wild disorder. Men ran blindly, flinging away weapons and equipment. "What had been an army ... was now a howling, screaming mob...." an eyewitness reported.

Pillow saw a chance to crush the Mexicans. Sending for Kearny, he pointed at the roadway with his sword, indicating the milling mass of Mexican soldiers. "Captain, I'm turning you loose on that rabble. Strike them with all your strength."

Philip was soon spurring for the Via San Antonio followed by Company F and a platoon from Captain McReynolds' command. The dragoons reached the road and made ready to charge. The roadway was almost completely blocked by abandoned Mexican baggage and ammunition wagons, jettisoned equipment and dead bodies. A loaded ammunition wagon caught fire and an explosion threatened. Such a blast would have wiped out the dragoons. Some New York infantrymen saw the danger, and disregarding their own safety, climbed the blazing wagon to hurl ammunition chests and gunpowder kegs into the river. Then the foot soldiers cleared the road of wagons to give the dragoons fighting room.

With the road open Kearny formed his men in pairs of fours and signaled the column forward at a gallop. The dragoons charged on, shouting and brandishing their sabers. The fleeing Mexicans were by then nearly two miles away. As the dragoons raced in pursuit Kearny was fifty yards in advance of them. Behind him pounded some 150 troopers.

About half a mile from the Garita San Antonio Abada, through which the road entered the city, Philip's men caught up with the retreating Mexicans.

Kearny was the first to strike the enemy. He slammed into the rear rank and then seemed to have been swallowed up in the mass of the enemy. The cavalrymen barreled in, slashing left and right with their sabers. A stricken shout went up from the Mexicans. *"Los gringos! Los gringos!"* they cried. Panic swept through the fleeing mob; men clawed and fought to get off the road and away from the terrible sabers, scattering in all directions. Many fled through the gateway into the city. Some flooded over the barricade and the two guns defending the *garita*, overwhelming the troops that might have been able to annihilate Kearny's men.

Had even one Mexican officer kept calm and rallied his men the American attack would have ended in a massacre of dragoons. But, apparently believing that the entire American Army was upon them, unnerved gunners opened fire into the mob pouring through the gate and grapeshot cut wide swaths in that thick throng.

General Scott was observing Kearny's charge, with Colonel Harney. The General grew fearful that the dragoons might be cut off and ordered Harney to have them recalled. Mounted trumpeters were immediately dispatched to sound the command. But amid the racketing guns, the shots and uproar, the repeated bugle calls were either unheard or unheeded by the head of Kearny's column. Those in the rear gradually obeyed the signal; small parties reluctantly dropped out of the chase and turned back. Kearny was soon left with but three or four pairs of fours. He was so intent on his charge that he did not realize what had happened to his command. With only a handful of followers he made for the San Antonio gate.

In Africa with the *Chasseurs* Kearny had learned the regiment's credo: "Charge! And when you hear the recall blown, it is not meant for you!" Far from the Algerian desert he now maintained that tradition. "I heard the trumpets," he admitted later, "but to the depths of my being I was a *Chasseur*. Those trumpets were not calling me...."

Kearny kept forward, straight to the *garita,* scattering Mexicans before him. The few dragoons who remained raced close behind him. In front of the *garita* the enemy had dug a wide ditch across the roadway. A participant described the scene:

...numbers of Mexicans had been pushed into the ditch by the pressure of the mass behind... but it was too wide for a horseman to jump... Perceiving that the Mexican mounted officers admingled with the flying crowd... abandoned their horses to make their way across the obstruction on foot... Kearny threw himself from the saddle... called upon his men to follow, dashed across the ditch and leaped into the midst of the Mexicans to enter the battery with them... In this audacious act he was nobly supported by two officers and a dozen dragoons....

According to Kearny's account of what next happened: "... our presence created confusion which never before or since have I seen equaled... Mexicans bawled, screamed and fell to their knees as though my men and I were superwarriors instead of mere soldiers... We formed ourselves in a circle, hacking and slashing with our sabers..."

All the Mexicans were not overawed by the dragoons, however. Within a few moments the enemy had realized that only a rash handful had attacked them and not a huge American force.

"Death to the gringos!" a mighty voice roared. Instantly the Americans had to fight for their lives as Mexicans swarmed on them. Dozens of hands clutched at Philip. He fought with such ferocity that he somehow broke loose.

In the struggle his leather baldrick, pistol belt and scabbard were torn off; his weapons had been wrenched from his hands. Mexicans and dragoons fought, cursed, yelled and grappled in the dust. All at once Kearny found himself free, stumbling along the road away from the gate. He ached from a dozen bruises; his nose gushed blood; his face was swollen and his head throbbed from a blow.

He began to run as the Mexicans at the *garita* opened fire on him. Bullets kicked up spurts of dust all around, but Philip was miraculously unscathed. The two field guns roared and grapeshot whizzed over his head.

He found a dragoon horse whose rider had been shot, swung into the saddle, and tried to spur the mount into a gallop but the animal was exhausted and could barely hobble.

Behind him the Mexican guns fired again. This time

the grapeshot did not pass harmlessly overhead. Now Philip was on horseback and more exposed than before. Shot shattered the bones of his left arm. The pain was intense but he managed to keep riding until he reached the American lines where he fell from the saddle.

Soldiers carried him to a dressing station and his left arm was amputated almost at the shoulder. While the surgeon worked, General Franklin Pierce—who would one day be President of the United States—held his head.

"Which arm have I lost, General?" the wounded man whispered.

"The left," Pierce said.

"I foresaw this," Kearny murmured.

His active service in the Mexican War was ended. In one bold charge he had won the glory he craved.

That evening General Scott came to his hospital tent to visit him. "I have this hour sent forward a dispatch mentioning your feat and putting in your name for a brevet to the rank of major," Scott told him.

All who had witnessed the action at San Antonio Gate concurred in the opinion that if Kearny had been properly supported Mexico City would have fallen before the day's end.

An officer on Scott's staff later stated:

Were Kearny followed by the number with which he had begun the charge ... or had no signal of recall been blown and he had been reinforced by infantry ... I believe Kearny would have made his way into Mexico City ... From the *garita* of San Antonio to the Grand Plaza is less than a mile and three-quarters ... and within that sector was not a single defensive work, and no organized defenders had there been any... All was indiscriminate panic, consequent confusion and flight... Unhappily, Kearny's charge went unsupported and the opportunity he had created with his audacity and boldness... went for naught but a glorious gesture....

BOOK THREE
1847–1862

"... *death, the sable smoke where vanishes the flame* ..."

CHAPTER XII

"I ASK no one's pity or sympathy..." Brevet Major Philip Kearny wrote his friend Cortland Parker. "You have made inquiry of my intentions as to the future. I shall remain in the Army performing those duties of which I am capable...."

He meant what he had written. When advised by the War Department that he was eligible for honorable retirement because of his physical disability Kearney told the Secretary of War: "I will not resign. I do not feel that my usefulness to the service is yet ended...."

He took a six-months disability leave and returned to New York City in December, 1847. Diana came from Paducah with the children and the Kearny's were again at home in New York. Another baby—Ann—was born in September, 1848.

KEARNY THE MAGNIFICENT

When his leave ended Philip was put in charge of the recruiting service in New York City. He confided to De Peyster: "I am most content as the master of my own establishment with my lovely garden which makes such a pleasant playground for my children...."

Despite this avowal he was not happy. The stump of his left arm healed slowly. At times he suffered extreme pain. Not even Diana knew what agonies he endured. When the attacks came he would lock himself in his study and remain there until the torture subsided.

His cousin Dr. Robert Watts warned him to "... refrain from violent exercises and not to attempt riding a horse for at least a year" lest the stump become inflamed and cause complications to develop.

Kearny took polite note of the doctor's instructions and disobeyed each of them. "I must strengthen my right arm to do the work of two," he said and hired a fencing master with whom he engaged in daily foil and saber matches. Always an excellent swordsman, he grew more adept than ever.

"The Major has the agility of a cat," the fencing master said. "I dare say he is even more agile. A cat lacking a paw would not move with his former speed. The Major is even faster than before his mishap."

Philip practiced lacing his boots, shaving and dressing, and exercised his right hand and arm for hours at a time. "The only real annoyance I have about losing my arm is the difficulty I have encountered in putting on my glove. Now, there's a challenge for a one-handed man!" Early each morning, whatever the weather, he went horseback riding and could soon manage any mount.

Unfortunately trouble erupted again between Kearny and Diana. They bickered and sulked like petulant children. They were too alike—both overly obstinate, arrogant and prideful. They loved in a destructive fashion, asking and taking too much from one another, and each was too haughty to yield or compromise.

A friend said of them: "Phil and Die are as flint to tinder. The flames grow too quickly. Soon nothing will remain but a cold, white ash."

The prediction was fulfilled. On August 24, 1849, Diana left New York, ostensibly to await the birth of her fifth child in Paducah. Another girl—Elizabeth Watts—was born there late in the year, but Diana never lived with her husband again. After only eight years the "perfectly matched" pair had reached the end of their marriage.

If Diana's departure shook Kearny he gave no evidence of it. He seemed unperturbed, although close friends knew that the breakup had hurt him keenly. Perhaps to cover up his real feelings he grew vitriolic over what he termed the "injustices" of his treatment by the War Department. He believed that his gallantry in the Mexican War had never been properly acknowledged, and complained bitterly that far greater honors had been awarded to other men for lesser deeds.

"I've heard of men who received two brevets for deeds which did not compare to my action at the San Antonio gate," he stated immodestly.

"No one could ever accuse Phil of humility. He craved fame . . . and was not one to hide his light under a bushel basket," a close friend observed wryly.

While the Government did not shower Kearny with medals and promotions, some prominent New Yorkers—members of the exclusive Union Club to which he belonged—demonstrated their appreciation of the "neglected" hero. On November 3, 1848, the club gave him ". . . a superb testimonial . . . for bravery in Mexico, especially at Churubusco. . . ."

At the sumptuous banquet "a magnificent sword" was duly presented. The blade was "a classic example of the swordmaker's art . . ." according to a newspaper account. In his presentation speech the chairman declared:

. . . you lost an arm in your country's service . . . now your friends and fellow townsmen are . . . desirous to testify their sense of your deserts by offering you an appropriate testimonial in honor of your noble bearing in that arduous campaign . . . Let this sword . . . when it reminds you of a war in which you shared alike the glories and the sufferings, be not valued the less since peace has followed the train of victory; nor yet let the weapon rust in its scabbard during a night of repose, lest another day should again summon you to the battle . . . Wear it in peace as in war, as a token of our admiration and your merit . . . Accept it as a testimonial from the friends whose esteem you possessed in . . . peace and who now acknowledge with pride your conduct in war. . . .

According to witnesses, ". . . tears were glistening in Kearny's eyes when he rose to reply. . . ." He said in part:

The sword of honor which I have received . . . is an overwhelming mark of distinction . . . For myself, when on returning from

Mexico... and arriving in my native city, I felt the pulse of sympathy beat high, and was received with cordiality by gentlemen whom I realize the honor of calling my friends and associates in the Union Club... my heart was touched... This day, on being presented with a sword of honor, I confess that my cup of ambition is filled to the brim... and that most amply am I repaid, whatever of peril and suffering I have encountered...."

The trophy somewhat mollified Kearny; it suited his vanity to know that if the quill-pushers in the War Department did not appreciate him, at least the more astute citizens of his hometown recognized a hero and knew how to treat one. His attacks on the "Washington bureaucrats" slackened and only rarely did he loose a blast against them after receiving the sword. He settled down to his recruiting assignment and did it so energetically that New York City soon had more enlistments than any other area in the military district.

CHAPTER XIII

In May, 1851, hundreds of New Yorkers were stricken with varioloid, a form of smallpox. The attacks reached near-epidemic proportions, especially in the city's slums. Health authorities warned everyone to shun the affected neighborhoods.

Kearny had established a recruiting station on Pearl Street in the Five Points district, a section which was to suffer badly in the epidemic. To the astonishment of his superiors he had achieved remarkable success in enlisting the young toughs of Five Points. The hard-bitten hoodlums who lived there gave Philip unconditional respect after he had horsewhipped a notorious local gangster who led the Water Rats—a band of river pirates.

The day the recruiting booth opened, the Water Rats

and their leader, Duster, attacked the sergeant and two soldiers on duty there. They would have burned the booth but for Phil who was just arriving. He leaped from his buggy, whip in hand, and sailed into the gangsters. He grabbed Duster and flung him into the gutter.

"Now, you scum, I'll beat some decency into you!" Kearny bellowed.

The buggy whip slashed down again and again until Duster screamed for mercy. His pals stood in a white-faced bunch; none of them moved to help Duster. He scuttled about in the gutter, throwing himself this way and that to escape the stinging whip, all the while bawling to his friends. But the Water Rats stood rooted, stricken with awe at Kearny's fury.

After a few moments, Duster managed to scramble away and lurched down the street, still shouting and bellowing. When he had gone, Kearny faced the rest of the hoodlums.

"Anybody else want the same dose?" he asked, brandishing the whip.

The young gangsters remained silent. Kearny turned his back on them, to glare at the sergeant and two privates who had manned the booth.

"Fine military specimens you are," the one-armed officer sneered. "You should have sent this rabble packing."

"Sir, they took us by surprise," the sergeant stammered.

"Enough, enough! I'll see you later. We have a job to do and that's to get ourselves some recruits," Kearny said. He looked over at the Five Points youths. "You're all supposed to be tough. Why don't you really prove it? The Army needs you! The Army needs men—even gutter rats like you! Come on, lads, chuck this life down here. Do your country and yourselves some good. Join up! That is, if you're men enough! Now, who'll be the first?"

There was confused movement among the gangsters and then a big, bushy-browed young man stepped out. "I'll sign the muster roll, Major—on one condition."

"What's that?"

"I want to shake your hand. Anybody that could clean up on Duster wins my vote. Will you shake?"

"My pleasure, sir." Kearny grinned and thrust out his hand.

Before the morning was over, a dozen Five Pointers had enlisted and from that day on, no further trouble took place at the recruiting station.

When the smallpox epidemic struck, Kearny still made his daily trip there though he had been advised to close the booth and avoid the vicinity. Learning that some of the new recruits had contracted the illness, he visited them in their squalid homes. The aristocratic officer must have seemed strangely out of place in these Five Points hovels. He entered foul basement dwellings and tenements where "... noisome odors ... make one retch ..."

Philip had never seen such poverty. He had probably not even been aware that conditions like these existed. "I was heartsick to witness human beings living in degradation ... grease, dirt and ordure were at every hand ... This was horror that shamed a battlefield ... I saw naked babies with putrescent sores covering their tiny bodies crawling on rotted floors where bloated rats slithered and scraped...."

Like his grandfather John Watts during the yellow fever plague in 1805, Kearny donated money, food and medicines to the sick men.

So deeply was he shocked by the horrors of Five Points that he said: "Were I the Supreme Power... I would erase these pestilential slums with a wave of my hand... It is the crime of our age to tolerate spawning grounds of crime, disease, degeneracy and death...."

He received an even greater shock when he spoke to fellow members of the Union Club about the slums. To his amazement he learned that several of them owned the very buildings he had visited and were well acquainted with their tenants' subhuman living conditions.

"... I wondered how these eminent and respectable men could sleep... Did not the wailing sick and hungry babies rise out of the festering slums to assail their ears? I saw my friends in a new light... They were civilized Christian gentlemen, not common knaves, and that made them even blacker villains in my opinion," Kearny wrote.

He was essentially a simple man who believed in the ancient chivalric code: the strong must aid the weak; the rich must help the poor. Philip knew that men lied, cheated and swindled for gain, but the revelation that his peers profited from the foul tenements was such a shock that he did not go to the Union Club for a long time and never again spoke to the men who owned the Five Points property.

Soon after he contracted varioloid, and was dangerously

ill for weeks. The sickness affected him in an odd manner—it left his face slightly pitted, and according to De Peyster, brought on a complete physical change. "Phil's body broadened, and from that time forward he developed and spread into the magnificent figure of a trooper. No longer was he built like a slight lad ... Fortunately, even though his cheeks were scarred, the blemishes in no wise detracted from his fierce good looks...."

After he had recovered, Kearny resumed his duties and kept at them for another year.

CHAPTER XIV

In July, 1851, Philip received orders to rejoin his old command in the First Dragoons at San Francisco. The assignment was welcome. After three years New York was becoming tiresome; perhaps he also believed it would be easier to forget Diana if he were 3,000 miles away from the city where they had lived. Another facet of the mission suited him as well. One of his business advisors had recently speculated in a California gold-mining deal and the venture had cost Kearny thousands of dollars; he hoped to recover the loss there.

The California gold rush was at its peak. Prospectors poured into the territory, coming by ship around the Horn and overland in covered wagons. Many died in the desert or on the mountain trails, few were lucky enough to find gold, and most gave up in despair or disgust. But the lust outweighed the perils and the hardiest pushed on to the coastal state.

Phil sailed from New York in August, 1851, and reached San Francisco a month later after a wearisome voyage to Panama where he had crossed the Isthmus and boarded a second ship on the Pacific side.

The First Dragoons were encamped south of the city. The unit's mission was to police the boom town and the nearby gold fields. It was no easy task. The dragoons were often forced to use sabers and gun butts to quell the many brawls and riots. Kearny had ordered his men to "crack down hard" on troublemakers, and the troopers carried out those orders with zest.

In a short time both San Francisco and the camps became noticeably more peaceful. Everyone saw Kearny meant business, and knew that it was better to obey his rules than violate them. Once the violence abated, Phil found time to look after his own affairs. He bought shares in a gold claim, and the stake proved rich enough for him to regain the money his agent had lost and to make a good profit. This coup convinced Philip that he was a shrewd investor. His friends knew that he had merely been lucky. He fortunately had no further opportunity to try his financial genius. His military duties took all of his time.

Early in the fall of 1851, the Rogue River Indians—a warlike tribe—had gone on a rampage. The braves blocked the direct north–south road that led from California into Oregon. Settlements were razed, farms destroyed, families wiped out. The smoke rose from burning cabins with heartbreaking frequency, and Joseph Lane—Governor of the Oregon Territory—appealed to the Army for help. It came in the form of a punitive expedition that included infantry, artillery and dragoons under Kearny's command.

He drove vigorously against the Indians, hounding the hostiles by pushing his troops long miles each day. The men complained that he was marching them too far and working them too hard, but Philip ignored the griping. "I shall continue to press the enemy... keeping him on the run until he must turn and do battle... when that time comes I shall destroy him... To accomplish this I shall do all I deem necessary... Shirkers and malingerers in my command will be regarded as deserters... and dealt with accordingly...." he announced to his troops.

They understood him. Desertion in front of the enemy meant a firing squad, and no one believed that Kearny would hesitate to have a soldier shot.

The grueling march continued. Horses, pack mules and men stumbled up rugged mountain trails in search of the Indians. Only Philip had energy left after even the hardest day; he was goaded by a fierce and obsessive drive for success. The men looked upon him with awe, grudging admiration and open dislike. Many years later one soldier said: "Nobody could figure out how the Major kept going... One armed as he was, he stayed in the saddle for hours without trouble... even when the march lay along mountain tracks that were dangerous and almost impossible for a two-armed man on horseback... yet he rode easily on paths that were difficult for a sure-footed mountain mule ... I can't say I liked him ... or that any of the other boys did ... but every one of us had to admit he was about the best officer in the Army...."

His dogged tactics brought results. The harried Indians turned to fight. About 300 Rogue River warriors made a stand at Table Rock. The braves had chosen a good defensive position with high ground and plenty of cover, but Kearny routed them in a series of spirited assaults. The weary dragoons and foot soldiers caught their commander's dash and scattered the Indians after inflicting many casualties. The demoralized braves fled across the Rogue River, the troopers pounding close behind.

At Evans Creek the hostiles again turned on their pursuers but were no match for Kearny who blasted them out of their rocky shelters with artillery. The engagement at Evans Creek terminated the Rogue River campaign. The Indians meekly returned to their hunting grounds and gave up marauding.

Governor Lane expressed the gratitude of all Oregon settlers in a letter to Philip: "... as an eyewitness to your movements and actions against the Rogue River Indians ... I can, with great truth, and do with no less pleasure, pay deserved respect to your gallantry as a soldier and ability as an officer ... I believe your feat in subduing the hostiles ... opened Oregon to peaceful settlement ... and I do now thank you for the great good you have secured this Territory...."

Following the short Rogue River War, Kearny brought Company F north to Fort Vancouver on the American side of the Columbia River. They met no hostile savages en route; the restive Oregon Indians had been subdued.

Philip was well pleased with the part he had played in this campaign. He had demonstrated that the loss of an arm had not impaired his military efficiency. Even more important, he had learned for himself that he was any man's physical equal despite the handicap.

Fellow officers praised, toasted and congratulated him. He basked in their homage and confided to a friend that his success would ". . . awaken those War Department deadheads to full recognition of my merit . . ." He smugly predicted that: "Soon I shall be wearing a lieutenant colonel's silver leaf . . . on my shoulder straps."

But this ambition remained unfulfilled. Kearny received no brevet nor even a commendation from Washington. After enduring several months of self-styled "humiliation" he went back to his old behavior pattern: sullen moods, flashes of anger, a biting vituperation against the Army hierarchy.

Although the inactivity that followed the Rogue River fighting began to irk him, Kearny appreciated California. "I like the splendid scenery and the balmy weather," he wrote a New York relative. But beautiful scenery was not enough. After fifteen years of service he yearned for high military rank. To a man such as Phil, rank epitomized both success and acceptance. He longed to reach the level of his Uncle Stephen who had died a major general in 1848.

This need for promotion possessed Philip. Aware that his financial and social positions had not been attained through his personal efforts, he wanted to achieve something on his own.

"I have wealth that I did not earn . . . I have never known a moment without money . . . In a way I envy those men who must daily struggle for economic survival . . . they can savor the smallest pleasures . . . while those born rich are dulled . . . by an overabundance of everything. . . ." Kearny once said.

No one took seriously his complaints about being wealthy. "At times Phil is inclined to wax philosophical . . . but I do not believe he would trade places with any man . . ." a friend remarked.

Cortland Parker seemed to have understood Kearny better than most: "Phil does not desire to live in poverty . . . he is no saint to give up his riches . . . all Phil wants is to rise to the heights by his own efforts in his chosen profession. . . ."

But Kearny received no further promotions. He was shunted from one post to another in California and assigned to various minor duties. He now began thinking of himself as a failure. To such a prideful man resignation seemed the only honorable course. This time no war loomed to rekindle his patriotic ardor. He saw nothing ahead but years of dull, colorless service. Phil believed that the War Department had overlooked him for promotion because he was not a West Pointer, and was convinced that the leading Army clique saw him as an outsider.

Probably he had justification for this opinion. Few officers who were not Military Academy graduates attained high rank during peacetime. In the regular Army, West

Pointers disdained colleagues who had not graduated from the Academy. Many of them undoubtedly envied Kearny. He had a superb combat record; he surpassed most of his superiors in background and wealth. Besides, the Mexican War had made him a national hero. With his youth, talent and ambition, Phil posed a threat to the mossbacks who ran the Army.

Although Winfield Scott, the Commander in Chief, recognized Kearny's value, not even he could squeeze out a promotion for his protégé. A Louisianian, Charles Conrad, was Secretary of War during Millard Fillmore's Administration and he dispensed promotions to his own favorites, especially Southerners.

Philip, caught up in the "old army game," lacked the two major qualifications for playing it—diplomacy and subservience. He now either had to truckle under and accept the actualities of the military or leave the Army for good.

He was sure of one thing. He could never endure the mossy obscurity to which so many captains and majors had been relegated. They shuffled papers at remote outposts, awaiting retirement with a desperate kind of patience. Kearny knew that such an existence was not for him. Instead, he submitted his resignation in October, 1851.

It was promptly accepted. "I had hoped for at least a token murmur of demurral," Phil said ruefully.

At thirty-six he found himself without a profession or family ties. The cares that burdened other men did not affect him. He had everything in life except a purpose.

For fifteen years the Army had provided him with one. Now that was over.

"Had I been as assiduously devoted to wife and children as I was to the Army... I would not today be rootless... *sans* spouse, *sans* offspring...." he wrote De Peyster in a depressed frame of mind.

CHAPTER XV

PHILIP's spirits were somewhat raised by the offer of a trip around the world aboard the U. S. S. *Vincennes* as the guest of her skipper Captain W. L. Hudson who had been ordered to "show the flag" in the remote Pacific and the Far East. Kearny eagerly accepted the invitation.

The *Vincennes* sailed from San Francisco on November 14, 1851, and was gone almost a year, putting in at places where Americans were seldom seen.

On October 10, 1852, the ship dropped anchor in New York and Kearny passed the fall and winter in that city. For the first time in years he could devote himself to Bellegrove, his property in East Newark, New Jersey, where he had decided to build a palatial home.

Before that project reached completion he again had a

touch of wanderlust. It was April, 1853, and he yearned for the broad boulevards and shaded streets of Paris, a city he called "... the ultimate achievement of Western civilization..." With no reason to stay in the United States, Kearny left for France and reached Paris on May 1. There he rented a magnificent house off the Champs Élysées at avenue de Matignon 15. He did not lack companionship, for even after thirteen years people still remembered the "best-known foreigner in France."

When he had been there about a month Philip was invited to a reception given at the Tuileries for English and American residents in Paris by Emperor Louis Napoleon III. Kearny attended the affair in his dragoon dress uniform, and a guest described him as "... the most magnificent man present..." He was presented to the Emperor by William Rives, the United States Ambassador. Louis Napoleon greeted him warmly and thanked him for his service to France during the Algerian War.

That day at the Tuileries, Philip met Agnes Maxwell, an auburn-haired American girl visiting in Paris with her parents. Her father, Hugh Maxwell, was Collector of Customs in the Port of New York. According to Kearny, twenty-year-old Agnes was "... an exquisite creature... so lovely that my eyes misted at her beauty..."

Agnes was no less impressed with him. After the Emperor's reception Kearny saw Agnes almost every day and realized that he had fallen in love with her.

"How incredible that this child... should hold such allure for me, a man old enough to be her father... This is a love of autumn and spring... I am nearing my fortieth year . . . she is barely twenty . . . I am married, have sired children, and she is affianced to a young man in New York . . . but I am mesmerized by her loveliness, gentleness and charm . . . I swear to you . . . nothing matters . . . neither gossiping tongues, the variance in our ages nor the obligations we have to others . . . for she feels about me as I do about her. . . ." Kearny wrote De Peyster in June, 1853.

He showered gifts on Agnes: perfumes, bon bons, jewelry, rare books, *objets d'art*. Every day he sent huge bouquets. They dined at celebrated restaurants, took long drives into the country, picnicked in the Bois de Boulogne, attended the races, and went boating on the Seine. Kearny's French friends were undisturbed by his attachment to Agnes, but unfavorable comment was created in the American colony.

Overriding her parents' objections, Agnes continued to see Philip and even broke her engagement to her New York fiancé. When she did that, Kearny resolved to marry her. In February, 1854, he returned to the United States and visited Diana in Paducah. He tried to persuade her that she should divorce him, but failed. Divorce was shameful and unthinkable to Diana; possibly she still hoped for a reconciliation. This did not suit Kearny and he returned to New York.

As a man of honor he now had to give up Agnes. He believed that she was still in Paris. But the Maxwells had returned shortly after his departure, and Agnes was in New York. When he discovered this Kearny fled the city to winter at Gouverneur without telling Agnes where he had gone.

"Perhaps she will think me a cad and forget that I even exist," he told a friend. "I must purge her from my heart ... else I shall lose my mind with longing for her ... ."

He lived in Gouverneur for several months while Agnes searched for him. Alone, except for a few servants, Kearny brooded constantly. He yearned for Agnes "... like a callow youth in the throes of first love ... ." but refused "... to subject my little girl of the Tuileries to the besmirchment which must needs follow any intimate relationship we might have. ... ."

When the winter's snow melted, Kearny resumed his daily horseback rides. He galloped far and fast over rough, treacherous ground still slippery from the recent thaw. Several times his mount stumbled and he managed to escape injury only by jumping clear as the animal fell.

As he fretted over the impasse with Diana and his need for Agnes the rides grew increasingly reckless. Phil seemed to be courting danger, and an accident appeared inevitable. One finally did occur, ironically not through his own doing. As he rode across Kearny's Bridge the old structure collapsed, hurtling horse and rider into the twenty-foot-deep gorge below.

Villagers carried the badly injured Kearny to Van Buren's Hotel in Gouverneur and sent for Dr. Robert Watts who was visiting his cousin. For a time Phil fought a seesaw battle with death, but eventualy began to recover. By September, Dr. Watts pronounced him fit enough to travel, and Kearny returned to New York in a specially rigged ambulance.

Watts found a comfortable apartment for his patient in the vicinity of Fourth Avenue and 23rd Street. A competent nurse was engaged, and Philip spent his days propped up on pillows at a window looking out on the formerly bucolic street.

The neighborhood had lost its rural atmosphere. Cross streets that had once appeared as grid lines on maps now actually bisected the city north of 34th Street. Only a few years before, sheep had grazed where wagons and carriages now rolled steadily by. Real-estate speculators were snatching up land all over Manhattan—even in the most remote districts at the northern tip of the island. The city was growing rapidly and already had more than a half-million inhabitants. Experts predicted that within twenty years the population would soar beyond a million.

Buildings were under construction all along Fourth Avenue and hammers clattered in the autumn air. Even the Rose Hill land had been broken up into lots and parcels; where the old farm had been, townhouses now marched in unbroken ranks. These changes saddened Kearny. He nostalgically remembered "... the solitude of the woodlands ... now vanished..."

Dr. Watts was not pleased with his patient's progress. "He seems to be fading ... I fear Phil has lost the desire to live ... I reluctantly draw this conclusion, for I can find no medical reason to account for his flagging condition ... Never have I seen him so constantly depressed...." the doctor noted in his journal.

As Kearny's decline continued Watts deduced that his patient was longing for Agnes, and went to see her. He told her what was happening. She was greatly distressed and insisted on being taken to Philip at once.

Disregarding Kearny's protests, Agnes paid him daily visits. She dismissed the nurse and took over his care. He soon showed improvement. The ring returned to his voice; his eyes sparkled; and by the end of October, Dr. Watts was able to discharge him as cured.

Agnes defied every convention of the times when she moved in with Kearny. She lived with him through the winter of 1854–1855, and in the springtime followed him to Bellegrove where she helped with the refurbishing of the estate. Work was rushed on the mansion overlooking the Passaic River. Kearny hired Frederick Law Olmsted, who had designed New York City's Central Park, to lay out the grounds at Bellegrove.

The spring of 1855 passed with the couple involved in the work at Bellegrove and with each other. "I have found with Agnes all the tranquility, happiness and contentment that one man could wish for in his lifetime...." Kearny said. Only Diana's intransigence about a divorce marred his happiness.

The house at Bellegrove had a medieval splendor. Olmstead created a private park modeled after the Luxembourg Garden in Paris. The estate became a showplace. "If Central Park is Olmstead's masterpiece, then Bellegrove is his second greatest work," a visitor commented.

Philip, an enthusiast in everything he undertook, decided to raise sheep and bought what experts called the finest flock of its size in the United States. But horses were still his chief delight and he took great pride in his thoroughbreds. His favorites were three matched grays named Moscow, Monmouth and Black Hawk.

The days on the huge estate were spent quietly. Kearny rode over his holdings, pausing to chat with gardeners, sheepherders and groundskeepers. It was during this period that he grew his distinctive Imperial beard after the style set by Louis Napoleon III. It pleased him to play the part of squire.

Kearny was so content that he refused a chance to act as an unofficial United States military observer of the Crimean War, which was then raging. He rejected an offer to accompany some army friends to the Crimea. "This is one conflict I must miss," Kearny explained. "After all, a man can't go to every war!"

Agnes was probably the reason he preferred to remain at Bellegrove. She had suffered a great deal through her love for him and was the target of much gossip. Kearny felt that she must not face it alone. Actually the ugly talk upset him far more than it did Agnes.

"Need I give ear to the cackling of hens or the yapping of mongrels? I love Phil, and presently this is the only way I can be with him. I have done nothing of which I am ashamed. . . ." she wrote a New York friend.

Her serenity infuriated the scandalmongers and they attacked her more viciously than ever. Kearny vowed that he would "slice out the tongue" of the first gossip he met "man or woman . . ." His threats brought no abatement to the torrent of slander, but eventually it died down as the busybodies found fresh objects for their venom.

While life at Bellegrove was pleasant enough, Kearny felt that a change would benefit them both. The new Russian Tsar, Alexander II, was to be crowned in St. Petersburg on March 2, 1856. All Europe was in a furor of excitement over the forthcoming coronation. Philip suggested that they enjoy the ceremonies at the Russian Capital and then make an extended tour of the Continent.

The couple arrived in France in January, 1856. They went to Rouen and rented an apartment at Rue Armand-Carrel 1, where they were known to all as Monsieur and Madame Philippe Kearny. After a brief stay in Rouen they proceeded to St. Petersburg for the coronation, which Philip described as a most "brilliant and elegant affair."

A leisurely trip through Europe followed with visits to the Continent's most important cities. On returning to Rouen, Kearny found messages from his New York agents urging him to come home—certain business matters required his presence in New York. He made a quick trip to Paris before sailing and bought the house at avenue de Matignon 15, hired a caretaker, and ordered the man to "... maintain this residence so that it will be suitable for immediate occupancy at all times."

Agnes and Philip were once again at Bellegrove in the early spring of 1857. Even after a year's absence a blizzard of disapproval still swirled about them. Whenever they appeared together tongues clacked and eyebrows were raised.

In August Diana went to New York for a visit. It was her first trip East in eight years and overzealous persons made certain that she was fully informed about her husband and the "Maxwell hussy."

The stories shocked Diana. She was a woman of pride and spirit and would not insist on holding a man who did not want her. Only the fact that Kearny had "taken a mistress" caused her to renounce her scruples against divorce. Having discovered the truth, she realized that her marriage was hopelessly destroyed and instructed her lawyers to file for divorce in New York. The proceedings stirred one of the ripest scandals the city had yet enjoyed.

The decree was granted in February, 1858. Diana returned to Paducah with the children and never again saw the man who had given her so little happiness.

Now Philip had his freedom. He envisioned the future as "... a beautiful existence with Agnes... a rhapsodic symphony without a note of discord..."

He and Agnes took the first available boat to France and were married in Paris at the house in the Avenue de Matignon. Agnes took her place as his wife with "great dignity" according to a Parisian friend. The Kearny home became a gathering place for the elite of the country. Philip's hospitality was princely and he soon regained his old reputation as the "best known foreigner in France."

The couple spent the rest of that year in complete happiness. According to Kearny, "... each day, indeed each moment with Agnes... I savored and enjoyed..." Together they explored Paris, finding splendid restaurants tucked away in obscure streets, discovering bookstalls and antique shops hidden in the city's nooks and crannies.

But the idyll could not last long in a troubled world. War again menaced at least a part of Europe. This time a conflict was brewing between Victor Emmanuel II, King of Sardinia, and Franz Josef, Emperor of Austria. Victor Emmanuel sought to unify Italy through driving the Austrians from Lombardy and the other regions of Italy which they occupied. He had arranged a treaty with Emperor Louis Napoleon which committed France to help him.

Hostilities between Sardinia and Austria broke out in April, 1859. In accordance with the treaty, the French mobilized to march with Victor Emmanuel. The marching troops, military bands and horses made Kearny restless. He stood on the balcony of his house and watched a squadron of *Chasseurs d'Afrique* trot past. "At that instant I knew he wanted nothing more than to join them," Agnes remembered.

"You are not to consider me," she told her husband, "but to do as your heart and spirit demand."

He did not hesitate long. "I am a soldier ... my second country—France—is in peril. What course can I pursue other than to fight for her as I have in the past?" he said.

CHAPTER XVI

KEARNY applied to General Morris, Commandant of Cavalry, whom he had known in Algeria, for a staff appointment. The General personally approved his request. By May 12, Philip was embracing his comrades of the *Chasseurs* at Alessandria, near Genoa, where a French Army of 150,000 men had congregated. To celebrate the reunion Kearny gave a banquet for his friends—an affair which a participant described as memorable.

The war was short and bloody. Actually only three major battles were fought—Montebello, Magenta and Solferino—but thousands fell in those clashes. The Battle of Montebello raged on May 20, as the French pushed north to Milan from Alessandria. Between May 31 and June 1, a series of minor engagements flared, and three days later a tremendous struggle erupted near Magenta. The French and Sardinians suffered serious losses in driving the Austrians from the field, but Louis Napoleon took Milan on June 7, and after some sharp fighting (June 9) pressed the enemy back to the Mincio River where the Austrians prepared for their final stand in Lombardy.

Since Kearny was attached to the Cavalry of the Guard, he took no part in any fighting, but as in Mexico, learned a great deal about strategy by watching the generals plan the campaign. Far greater numbers of troops were involved than Scott had employed twelve years earlier on the long march from Vera Cruz to Mexico City.

The Battle of Solferino was fought on June 24. The Austrians, with 160,000 men, were advancing to attack, while the French and Sardinians, numbering 150,000, had also launched an offensive. The two armies met head-on near the Mincio River and skirmishing commenced at 5:30 A.M. on a muggy day, already stiflingly hot even at that early hour. The fighting soon spread into a general engagement along a twenty-five-mile front that stretched in a southerly direction from Lago Garda on the left to Castel Gofreddo on the right.

The Austrian center was anchored at Solferino, a small town some five miles west of the Mincio. Franz Josef's troops held splendid positions on high ground to the west of that village. At 7 A.M.—an hour and a half after the battle had begun—Louis Napoleon, directing the operations of his army from a command post in the church steeple of nearby Castiglione, ordered a frontal assault on Solferino.

The French infantry gallantly responded to the Emperor's command but was pounded to a standstill by artillery and rifle fire from the entrenched Austrians. Brigade after brigade charged cheering to destruction with fixed bayonets behind regimental flags.

The terrible attack went on all morning until "... the ground was littered with corpses ... the parched earth soaked in blood ... The flower of France was sacrificed at Solferino. ..." as a war correspondent reported.

The casualties finally affected the morale of the attacking soldiers; reserves marched grudgingly to the front. Rumors of panic in the French rear aroused resentment among the shock troops. "Those swine are leaving us to die while they save their own skins," a powder-grimed soldier cried.

The assaults on Solferino grew weaker, and the dispirited Frenchmen "no longer charged with dash and *élan*," an eyewitness observed. Then at about 2 P.M. wild cheers rose from the Infantry marching up toward Solferino. "The cavalry! The cavalry!" men shouted, pointing to the west. Everyone turned as *Chasseurs,* dragoons, lancers, and cuirassiers arrayed in a long column of squadrons came up at full trot, raising "thick, choking dust clouds ..." The mounted units had been rushed from positions almost sixteen miles away and had come to make "a final effort to rout the Austrians ..."

As the French cavalry approached the battle line thunderclouds gathered and lightning flickered. General Morris rode at the head of the horsemen followed by his staff; Phil

Kearny in full United States Dragoon uniform, cantered at the General's side. Riders and horses were powdered with white dust; everyone was hot and tired. But when the bugles signaled the cavalrymen to form in assault ranks personal discomfort was forgotten. Exultant yells rose from thousands of throats, and even before the last notes had faded, the troopers were galloping into position.

It was an "unforgettable spectacle," a participant remembered. Uniforms of scarlet, white, blue and green merged into a colorful patchwork, while the flags, pennons and banners were brilliant against the darkening afternoon sky.

"The long lines stretched in perfect array . . . suddenly, an expectant hush fell upon the battlefields. The guns stopped . . . even the horses stood motionless, and only the faint cries of the wounded broke the magical silence. . . ." wrote a staff officer.

While the troops were deploying, Kearney asked General Morris for permission ". . . to go forward, the better to witness the action about to be undertaken by my old comrades of the *Chasseurs.* . . ."

"I could not deny you that pleasure." The General smiled.

A moment later the one-armed American was galloping swiftly toward the sector occupied by the *Chasseurs*. He brought his horse to a rearing stop as they greeted him, brandishing their sabers and emitting shrill Arab war cries. Kearny had barely jockeyed his horse into line when the lull was shattered by Austrian guns. Shells exploded around the cavalry. Bits of shrapnel whizzed like angry wasps. Volleys of rifle fire flamed from the hill in front of them.

French cannon replied, and shellbursts mushroomed along the ridge. Suddenly a trumpet sounded; then another—the signal for the *Chasseurs* to charge.

"As one the line leaped forward... the desert veterans gave the bloodcurdling, ululating war whoops of the Arabs and raced at the enemy... across the broken ground they sped... but not even the fleetest could keep up with Phil Kearny, bridle in his teeth, saber flourished overhead..." recalled an infantry officer who had watched the attack.

The Austrians held only long enough to pour a few volleys into the ranks of the charging cavalry. Men toppled and riderless mounts ran along with the charge. In moments the yelling horsemen had swept up the slope and driven the Austrian infantry in disorder. As they reached the enemy, General Morris rushed in squadron after squadron of lancers, dragoons and cuirassiers. The Austrian center collapsed. Men who had been fighting courageously only minutes before now fled in panic. The French infantry followed to occupy the heights of Solferino, and the cavalrymen returned to their own lines. It had been a magnificent charge but a costly one.

The *Chasseurs* alone had 27 officers killed. Hundreds of Frenchmen were lost, but that onslaught practically ended the battle, although fighting continued until 4 P.M. when a torrential thunderstorm broke over the battleground. The Austrians retreated across the Mincio River in the rain. The day had cost them 22,000 casualties, while the

French and Sardinians had paid for their victory with 17,000 dead and wounded.

General Morris scolded Kearny for his reckless daring, but took the bite out of his words by adding, "I have cited far less valorous men for the cross of the Legion of Honor..."

About two weeks after Solferino, Emperor Louis Napoleon met Emperor Franz Josef at Villafranca on July 10, and the two rulers concluded a peace treaty. Philip, who had returned to Paris, wrote De Peyster on July 14:

My two months' absence has been all that a military man could have desired... I have roamed about everywhere, and in the day of Solferino... I was present with the line of our cavalry skirmishers... That day I was mounted from six in the morning until eleven at night—scarcely off my horse even for a few minutes—depend on it, he was a good one. The cavalry of the guard came up some sixteen miles at full trot and rapid gallop to take our places under fire... The night before the battle I had a miraculous escape, having been inveigled by false guides into the midst of the Austrian masses... Once I saw the deception, I spurred to safety under a hail of Austrian lead ... Paris is very warm... more so than I have ever known it, and my health, which had been excellent, broke down when I arrived here... However, I am now on the mend....

Kearny had been in Paris only a few days when Agnes revealed a welcome secret; the doctors had confirmed the fact that their baby could be expected in January, 1860.

"I am the happiest man in France—no, in the world!" Philip exulted.

He decided that Paris in the summer was no place for

Agnes and rented a chalet on the shores of a lake in the Swiss Alps, hiring a retinue of servants to staff the retreat.

Shortly before they were to leave for Switzerland, Kearny received an imperial order to appear at Fontainebleau where the Emperor was holding court. The summons specified that he was to come in uniform.

A surprise awaited him there. He was escorted to the Emperor's chambers where the Cavalry Commander, General Morris, and a dozen officers of the *Chasseurs* were with Louis Napoleon. The Emperor greeted Philip warmly and then explained the purpose of the gathering. General Morris had cited him for gallantry at Solferino, and Louis Napoleon intended to award "... the brave American the Cross of the Légion d'honneur for the second time; the only foreigner ever to be so decorated for military service to France...."

The medal was bestowed; the accolade given. Philip's friends crowded around to congratulate him. His eyes glistened and his voice was husky with emotion as he said, "I am honored beyond words... this is my proudest moment..."

Later in July the Kearnys went to Switzerland and remained at the chalet until the end of September.

That autumn and winter very little formal entertaining took place at avenue de Matignon 15. Agnes solemnly awaited the birth of her child, while Philip railed against the "damnably slow parade of the days." He fumed impatiently until Agnes laughed. "You must remember, Major, that a baby's birth is not a military maneuver. You cannot order a child to be born at your convenience!"

The time came on Wednesday, January 25. Agnes bore a son who was named Archibald Kennedy Kearney after his father's long-dead great uncle, a prominent New Yorker. Philip acted like a young husband celebrating the arrival of his first child. Every member of the household staff was given a generous sum of money and each caller at their home during the week following the birth—whether friend, neighbor, tradesman or errand boy—received a watch as a celebration token of Archibald's birth. Kearny wrote De Peyster: "... our son is handsome, sturdy and well formed ... I pray he will enjoy a grand life, and I thank God for having blessed my middle years with such a perfect offspring."

Affairs finally settled down at the Kearny house. Archie flourished so well that his father could remark, "... he is blooming like a flower ..." Once more Paris society flocked to avenue de Matignon 15 as the Kearnys resumed their entertaining. But the gaiety of these events was dampened by the sharpening crisis in the United States. Secession, slavery and States' rights were hotly argued in the Kearny drawing room; the guests included Americans residing in Paris or visiting there. Sometimes voices grew loud, and on one occasion fists flew during a heated discussion.

Kearny ardently supported the Union, and since his views carried weight with influential Frenchmen—especially in military circles—his opinions helped counteract the voluble Southern sympathizers seeking to gain French favor. Advocates of the Northern viewpoint were in the minority; most Americans in Paris sided with the South. According to a contemporary journalist, the reason was that: "... the bulk of Americans resident abroad possess but little influence ... either from intelligence, culture or distinction of any kind ... They are chiefly people of good incomes who left home because they found themselves—or at least imagined themselves—of more consequence abroad. It ... is their style to affect sympathy with the Southerners as representing the more aristocratic side...."

It was a paradox for Kearny to back the Union cause. By taste, temperament and breeding, he had an affinity for upper-class Southerners, and often admitted preferring the gracious elegance of Charleston, for example, to the Yankee way of life. He believed in "aristocracy," as did the Southern "gentry." To him the highest human virtues were chivalry and courage. Yet he detested slavery and slave-owners. The "peculiar institution" was, he felt, "an inhuman practice and a barbarous evil."

"No man has the moral right to own another human being. I say slavery is despicable! I would see it damned to hell! It is a stain on the American flag!" he had once shouted at an officer who was defending his family's slaveholding.

The hour was coming when logic, reason and wit could not settle the rift between North and South. The United States was being torn apart, and three thousand miles away in France, Kearny predicted that his country would soon be wracked by "...a cruel and ugly civil war... The hatreds between North and South can only be washed away in blood...." He made this grim prophesy to an officer in the French Army.

"I weep for your benighted country." The Frenchman sighed.

"So do I," Philip replied. "When the hour comes I shall fight to preserve the laws, the integrity and the existence of my native land. I shall draw my sword once more. This time not against an alien foe, but my own brothers."

He evoked a promise from a homeward-bound New York businessman who later wrote: "Phil and I parted in Paris in 1860 ... I remember his last request was to let him know the state of affairs in the United States ... As soon as the secession of the Southern states appeared inevitable I informed him to that effect and received for answer ... that he would come back at once should war break out ... and offer his services to the national Government ... He concluded by saying that he had no trust or confidence in Southerners ... even if they should succeed in establishing their independence, as there was nothing practical about them ..."

The year 1860 dragged to its conclusion. In November, Abraham Lincoln won the Presidency, and the parade of secession began. Darkness fell on the nation as hope vanished.

In early April 1861 the holocaust struck. It came with a roar of cannon at Fort Sumter. The barrage echoed across the Atlantic, and men shuddered at the calamity that had befallen America.

The news reached Philip as he and Agnes breakfasted on

their terrace. A courier from the French War Ministry told them that civil war had started in America.

"Phil turned pale," Agnes remembered. "When he set down his cup I noted that his hand trembled. Never before had I seen him so unnerved. 'My God! They have all gone mad!' he exclaimed. He then became very calm. 'My dear, you understand that we must leave for New York at once,' he said. I nodded . . . tears blurred my vision . . . I thought, my poor country, my poor Phil. . . ."

The Kearnys dismantled their Paris establishment and had everything put in storage. "We shall live here again," he assured Agnes, "when the conflict is over. My country needs me. The Government will want experienced officers to train and lead the raw troops. This will be a long war. I know the Southerners. They will fight to the death. Every city, town and village will have to be taken at bayonet point. The South has gambled its traditions, its past, its future—its very life—on this adventure. Either they or we shall triumph, and no matter who wins, America will never again be as we have known and loved her."

Matters progressed too slowly for Philip. His desire to get home and "take part in this accursed war" became obsessive. He regarded every minor delay as a personal affront. He railed at the packers and movers for wasting time; then mollified the men with huge tips. He created a stormy scene at the steamship company office over their accommodations.

Agnes recalled how ". . . Phil stomped about, beard bristling, eyes flashing, shouting orders to do this and to do that until I brought him up short by saying sharply, 'Have no fear, Major! The war will last until you get home!' Knowing Phil as I did, I guessed he was apprehensive that the hostilities might come to a speedy conclusion ere he played a role in them... although I knew he had spoken otherwise... but my words had an effect. His behavior underwent an abrupt change and he quieted down considerably."

CHAPTER XVII

THE Kearnys arrived in New York during the last week of April, 1861, to find the city boiling with war fever. Flags flew everywhere—from rooftops and windows in schools, factories and public and private buildings. No day passed without martial music accompanying the tread of marching men as more and more state regiments tramped down Broadway from armories and drill halls to entrain or take ship for the journey to Washington. The streets teemed with people. Traffic was thicker than ever. Hotels, restaurants, saloons and theatres had never been so prosperous.

Despite the stir and bustle, Kearny's arrival was not ignored. All of the newspapers carried announcements of his return, and word that the Hero of Churubusco had come home caused a flurry in New York society.

The gossip that had raged about Kearny and Agnes was revived with zest, but Philip had little time to bother with whispers concerning his private life. As soon as Bellegrove could be prepared for them he installed his family there and left for Washington.

Fully expecting an important command and a general's rank, he offered his services to Secretary of War Cameron. But no offer came. Kearny was shunted from one official to another. Each received him politely and announced that unless he would take a subordinate post—since field-grade and general officers had already been selected—no place was available in the Regular Army.

"Even if such rank had to be filled, it is doubtful that you would be a candidate for it. Disabled and handicapped as you are, I am dubious that you would be acceptable. After all, we don't expect one-armed men to fight our battles," a high War Department official told him bluntly.

Kearny was outraged. "I have more firsthand knowledge of warfare than that pompous ass Cameron or any of the fools surrounding him!" he cried in protest. "With one arm gone, I am a better soldier than those who treat me so cavalierly!"

He was bitterly convinced that the West Point clique was persecuting him. In characteristic style he expressed this suspicion with force and vigor. He made known his opinions of Cameron, the War Department, the people who ran it, and the hidebound Regular Army "mossbacks" in charge of defending the country. Phil felt they were heading for a "military debacle" with their "outmoded training methods and creaky strategy... They underestimate the enemy's courage, skill and potential... They are ignorant of the truth. Many of the Army's best officers are with the Rebels... yet the leaders of the Government appear to be content with second best... This attitude can only result in disaster for our cause...."

Such statements did not make him popular with the military. But the bigwigs in Washington had offended him. Hurt and angry, Kearny was striking back at them, even though he knew that every derogatory remark he uttered lessened the possibility of his obtaining a suitable command.

A friend suggested that since there was great need for qualified men to organize and train the troops being raised by the various states, the Governor of New York might be receptive to "a native New Yorker who is a noted soldier as well... and could be induced to pin a star on such a person..." Since the Northern States were appointing brigadier and major generals "in proportion to the numerical strength of the forces organized within their jurisdictions," Kearny felt that he would stand a better chance in Albany than in Washington.

He decided to apply for a general's rank in New York State and was aided in this by General Winfield Scott who had vainly sought a Regular Army post for his former aide. But not even Scott's influence had budged the War Department, and the aged General now urged Phil to approach Governor Edwin Morgan of New York.

Scott wrote Morgan:

I beg leave to suggest Major Philip Kearny of New York, late a distinguished officer of the Army, for a high commission in the New York Volunteers. Major Kearny's long and valuable experience in actual military service seems to commend him as a useful as well as a valuable commander and disciplinarian. He is among the bravest of the brave and of the highest military spirit and bearing...

Armed with Scott's warm testimonial, Philip proceeded to Albany. He was not able to see the Governor, being blocked by politicians who had their own favorites for the dozen or so generalships available. The objections raised to Kearny's appointment ranged from his politics—he was a Democrat, the Governor a Republican—to the charge that "... a divorced man is not a fit leader for decent young Americans to follow...."

Between the bluenoses and the ward heelers Philip was frozen out when the one-star and two-star ranks were filled, although on his record alone he merited an appointment.

The Governor's treatment of Kearny kicked up protests, and one leading newspaper editorialized: "Those who objected to Major Kearny on moral grounds are sanctimonious fools... Those who opposed him for political reasons are idiots... Few men have seen more active service than he... It is pitiful that such a man is rejected at a time when we so sadly need experienced officers without a taint of treason...."

However, political expediency outweighed military logic. "No one in New York State's Government seems to care whether or no our newly made generals are good soldiers. The lives of our fine young men are of less importance than the wishes of ward heelers and political leaders whose protégés have to be given consideration...." grumbled a disgusted New Yorker who had supported Kearny's claims.

"It is scarcely to be believed," noted John Watts De Peyster in a letter "that Phil was passed by in favor of individuals who had no more to recommend them than the presumption with which they offered . . . their applications . . . and the want of principle with which those applications were pressed and backed by self-seeking politicians. . . ."

Attorney Cortland Parker was not surprised at the results of his friend's efforts. "I have had practical experience in politics and knew at the outset that Phil had little chance. His nature did not sit well with politicians. He took affront at every attempt to dwarf the grand conflict into anything less than a struggle for sublime principles. He had no faith in politicians, little respect for dignitaries, no love for anything but the cause. . . ."

Disgusted and disillusioned, Kearny turned from Albany. "I have been traduced by intriguers," he said. "What am I to do? I have traveled three thousand miles to serve my country. I would enlist as a private, but with one arm I am patently physically unable to fight in the ranks. Surely in this grave crisis my years in the Army, my experience both at home and abroad, will not be wasted."

Apparently his career as a soldier was over; his dream of winning new glory in the Civil War seemed ended. But he was not forgotten by everyone. A group of wealthy and patriotic New Yorkers had formed a regiment—the First New York (Lincoln) Cavalry—soon after the firing on Fort Sumter. The members equipped themselves at their own expense with superb horses and fine weapons. Each man was an excellent rider and a crack shot.

Bayard Clark, a prominent New Yorker, was elected Colonel of the elite regiment. He went to Washington and proudly offered his troop to General Scott who refused to muster the Lincoln Cavalry into Federal Service.

"I shall crush this rebellion in short order with the regulars under my command," Scott imperiously told Clark. He was willing to accept volunteer infantry regiments for "garrison duty" but saw no need for additional cavalry. Even the nation's first soldier did not fully understand the nature of the war.

Colonel Clark furiously left Washington, resigned from the troop, and was heard from no more. The unhappy men of the Lincoln Cavalry cast about for a new colonel. Someone suggested Kearny. Still smarting from his rebuffs in Washington and Albany, Phil accepted quickly.

Despite his reputation as a cavalryman, the Government still refused to muster in the Lincolns. Once again Kearny floundered in red tape and shortsighted military planning.

"Don't be downhearted," he told the troop. "One day very soon they'll come begging you to fight and save their scrawny necks. Despite the mossbacks you shall yet serve your country!"

His speech satisfied the men, but he admitted: "I would that I believed my own words."

While Phil "stewed and chafed; fretted and raged; fumed and ranted" over his own inactivity and while "nobodies, nincompoops and incompetents" were winning rank and position, a prominent New Jersey resident—J. C. Jackson—learned that the First New Jersey Brigade needed a commanding officer. Several men had tried to lead the brigade but could not cope with the rough and disorderly Jersey volunteers.

Jackson advised Governor Charles S. Olden that Kearny could do the job. "He is not only a grand soldier, but one of this State's leading citizens..." Jackson pointed out.

Kearney's friends organized a determined campaign to get him the command. They had undertaken a difficult task. Politicians swarmed around Governor Olden, pressing him to accept their particular candidates. The Governor hesitated for weeks without committing himself to any man. His instincts told him Philip was the candidate best qualified, but he was under great pressure to reject the one-armed soldier.

Olden's dilemma was solved on July 21, 1861. The North was shocked to learn of a great Southern victory at Bull Run, Virginia—the first large-scale engagement of the war. The defeat had resulted from the unskillful handling of troops by inexpert officers. As Kearny had predicted, War Department bungling had brought on a military disaster.

Volunteer regiments and Regular Army troops had fought well enough, but the grand march south—heralded as an attack "to annihilate the Secessionists"—turned into a shameful fiasco. Politically appointed officers had run away in disgraceful fashion, abandoning their inexperienced men, most of whom had never "heard a shot fired in anger" before the battle. As one observer said, "... it was not surprising that the battle was lost ... the amazing thing was that the men fought at all...."

The disastrous conclusion to the Battle of Bull Run

shook the War Department bureaucrats and made President Lincoln aware that high commissions could no longer be handed out to nonentities for political reasons. The outcome of Bull Run also prodded Governor Olden to a decision.

"I do not intend that my bold Jersey lads shall be sacrificed on the field of battle because they are led by inept weaklings," he announced. With that he offered the brigade to Kearny.

The choice was not easy for Phil. Just as Olden's bid had come, word had arrived that the Lincoln Cavalry would soon be mustered into Federal service for active duty. The men of the Lincolns had learned to depend upon Kearny and he was reluctant to leave them. But he preferred command of an infantry brigade rather than a cavalry regiment; the former called for the rank of Brigadier General, the latter only a colonelcy.

The dilemma was resolved when Kearny secured another commanding officer for the cavalry troop—Colonel Alexander T. McReynolds—who had taken part in the charge at Churubusco, emerging from that fray with a permanently crippled left arm.

"McReynold's wing is clipped too," Kearny said. "But he is one of the greatest cavalrymen in the land."

The Lincolns were satisfied with their new colonel, and Philip felt free to take on the New Jersey Brigade. One hurdle remained before he could be mustered in as its Commanding Officer. President Lincoln must sign the commission appointing him to that grade in the United States Volunteers. When Kearny's name came before him

Lincoln said, "I knew the man when he was a Mexican War captain. I know his record. He is my Brigadier. No one shall be appointed before him." With that the President affixed his signature to Kearny's commission which was dated July 27, 1861—retroactive to May 17, and placed him twelfth on the list of brigadier generals.

The following day Philip was ordered to take over the First New Jersey Brigade, Franklin's Division, Army of the Potomac, then in camp at Alexandria, Virginia. Before leaving he had transferred funds to Agnes and seen to it that she would be comfortable at Bellegrove.

The First New Jersey Brigade (First, Second, Third and Fourth New Jersey Volunteers plus a battery of field artillery) was encamped on the grounds of Fairfax Seminary in Alexandria.

The outfit lacked discipline, its morale was low, the men were sullen and insubordinate. The camp site was a disgrace. "Our encampment lacks the crudest sanitation ... the food is dreadful and the tents are like pig sties," a volunteer wrote home. "We need someone to make us into soldiers ... until now we've been having a big thing ... drinking, gambling, fighting and raising hell. ..."

After a look at his troops Kearny said: "... my first impression of this brigade is most unfavorable ... These are not soldiers, but a mass of slovenly men ... unruly, unwashed, untrained ... I am shocked at the conditions I have found ... but those wild lads are in for an even greater shock ... I shall make soldiers of them. I swear it!"

Phil arrived at the camp in mufti; the brigadier general's

uniform he had ordered had not been ready. A short walking stick tucked under the stump of his left arm, the new General strode through the camp gate, which had been left unguarded.

Drunken soldiers staggered about the littered company streets. Whisky-hoarse voices argued, shouted, cursed and laughed raucously. Kearny glared at a group of officers standing outside the guard tent, passing around a bottle of whisky. He charged up to them, gripped the walking stick in his good right hand, and smashed the bottle with it. An officer who was present recorded what followed.

"What sort of officers are you?" he bellowed, "to behave like loafers and drunkards before your men?"

"Who the devil are you, mister?" an officer asked. "You can't come barging in here like this, busting our bottle, and you only a civilian to boot."

"Is that your Headquarters?" Kearny asked, pointing to a small frame house.

"And what if it is?" the officer said belligerently.

"Shut up, Charley," another lieutenant warned. "This is Phil Kearny."

"The General?"

"Yes! The General!" Kearny cried. "I'll handle you! I want each of you to report at Headquarters in five minutes, properly dressed. Five minutes, you understand!"

With that he marched stiffly toward the Headquarters building. "You could practically see the smoke rising out of him . . . he was so mad. . . ." the writer reported.

The officers presented themselves at the specified time. Kearny delivered a biting lecture on the duties of officers.

The uneasy men listened silently until it was over. Then one spoke for the group: "If the General wishes, each one of us will resign," he said.

"Resign? That's the easy way! You need leadership, that's all!" Philip held up his right fist. "Well, gentlemen, this is the hand that will tame you. I hold a tight rein and I mean to make the First New Jersey the best brigade in the Army! Will you help me?"

"Yes!" the officers cried eagerly.

"Good. Now it's time we were properly introduced," Phil said.

"From that moment . . . every man . . . understood that a new day had come. . ." the officer's story continued. "Phil Kearny was hell bent to perfect the brigade . . . even if he had to run us all into the ground to do it," he confided.

A new day had indeed dawned for the First New Jersey. The rollicking, rowdy time of the past was ended. Within days of Philip's arrival radical changes took place. The General seemed to be everywhere at once. He would arrive at the mess tent at mealtime and sample the food. If it did not meet with his approval someone felt his wrath.

The camp underwent a complete transformation. Tents were aligned, latrines dug, work details and fatigue parties organized. A rigid training schedule was drawn up and Kearny made certain that it was followed. The sounds of roistering were replaced by noncoms and drill sergeants shouting commands. There was endless practice of combat maneuvers by squads, companies and regiments. From reveille until tattoo every man was busy every minute.

"Kearny accomplished nothing less than a military miracle in transforming the First New Jersey from a brawling, riotous rabble to a sharply trained organization," an observer stated.

"Kearny works us like field hands... He don't let up for a minute... He's hard on the men, all right... but I'll say that he's a sight harder on the officers... I'd sooner be caught in the jaws of a lion than to be a shoulder strap the general finds botching his job...." a soldier in the Second New Jersey Regiment said.

Sometimes Philip was brusque: sometimes his severity even bordered on eccentricity. But when the men saw that he was less willing to forgive a mistake made by a "shoulder strap" than one committed by a private they realized his actions were for the good of all.

Both officers and men found that the only way to satisfy him and avoid punishment was by the scrupulous performance of duty. When this was understood the brigade learned another side of its Commander. He was quick to praise a job well done.

He had soon weeded out unsuitable officers, demoted inefficient noncoms, and replaced them with deserving men. "So keen is the General's judgement of his subordinates that he rarely makes an error in sizing up a man; those he has elevated seldom belie the trust he has placed in them," Corporal Alfred Walters, Second New Jersey Volunteers, wrote his parents.

The General knew how to impress soldiers; he knew what appealed to them. "Man, horse, uniform, gesture and tone were all in keeping. He insisted that his staff and orderlies be attired elegantly. He even had a bugler boy dressed in a special uniform and mounted on a pony accompany him everywhere, like a knight and his page. The General's boots and leather had to be well polished; his brass and steel shining like burnished gold and silver ... Phil Kearny was a soldier's soldier," an officer who served on his staff said many years after the war.

Sparks flew where Kearny turned up. The men cheered whenever he rode through camp. "He transmits energy like a galvanic battery!"

It was not long before Kearny became a legend in the Army of the Potomac. His own men told how he had once ridden out at night to inspect a front-line guard post. The officer turned out the guards who had just come off duty and drew them up to attention for the General.

"Confound it, Lieutenant!" Phil scolded, "stop this paradeground nonsense! These men may have to fight the enemy in the morning. They need sleep more than I need salutes."

The General lived well in the field. A luxurious wagon, its interior completely carpeted and upholstered, followed him everywhere. It had an ice chest filled with French wines. A field kitchen, supervised by a Parisian chef who prepared his meals, was a part of his entourage. He paid for all this himself, of course. It was rumored that he had twenty tailored uniforms and two dozen pairs of handmade riding boots.

His soldiers loved to boast about their colorful General. Certainly no brigade had a more dashing commander.

"He's the top Brigadier in the whole Army," a private said. "And if he ain't, at least he's the richest!"

When Kearny assumed command of the brigade, the Confederates—under General Joseph Johnston—had their main base at Centerville, Virginia, near the old Bull Run battlefield, about thirty-five miles from Washington. The Rebels' advance positions reached to Munson's Hill, some six miles northwest of Alexandria. The enemy flag atop the hill could be seen plainly from the Union lines. The First New Jersey Brigade held the sector closest to the Confederate front. Kearny's pickets occasionally skirmished with the Southerners.

The Union Commander in Chief, George B. McClellan, felt that the New Jersey troops were too exposed, and ordered a withdrawal to a "safer area." "I am holding the outworks of our lines, forging my brigade in the presence of the enemy. What better training can I afford my men than to keep them constantly on the watch, alive to the fact that any hour they must fight?" Kearny argued with his superior.

Finally General McClellan reluctantly consented to let Phil hold the forward position. Every day the one-armed General eyed the Confederate flag on Munson's Hill. "I shall pay fifty dollars to the man who tears down that banner of treason," he promised. Months were to go by before he had the satisfaction of seeing the Stars and Stripes and not the Stars and Bars fluttering over Munson's Hill. The summer of 1861 passed without a decisive move by either side.

McClellan's army spent the autumn in drilling and more drilling; training and more training. This routine was periodically broken by parades and reviews. McClellan—the Young Napoleon, his admirers called him—had a taste for such spectacles. He loved to watch his divisions pass in perfect alignment, every eye watching as he took the salute.

McClellan was a dashing figure who resembled Kearny in many ways. He had wealth, social position and charm, and exuded confidence. He delivered speeches that evoked cheers but had yet to fight and win a major battle, although early in 1861, he had gained acclaim for driving Robert E. Lee and his Rebels from the western part of Virginia.

Little Mac, as the men affectionately dubbed him, gave the despairing North new hope after Bull Run. He had efficiently reorganized the shattered troops and forged the Army of the Potomac—a magnificent host of more than 100,000 strong and splendidly equipped soldiers. It was an army "whose equal had never been seen in the Western world." The Army of the Potomac, Little Mac boasted, was "the giant sledge hammer that would soon pound the Confederacy to dust."

But even though the regiments were drilled to razor-edge sharpness and no army had ever seemed more ready to fight a foe, McClellan did not march. Instead he hesitated and equivocated. He had all of the qualities of greatness except one—audacity. There his resemblance to Phil Kearny ended. Kearny dared, and while he usually succeeded, was not afraid to take the responsibility for failure. The Young Napoleon had to be assured of success. He developed a timidity that did not jibe with his martial façade. As a result of his need for assured success, McClellan met with failure.

He let the autumn slip away without undertaking any important move. It was a wasted opportunity, because during the fall the dirt roads of Virginia were in good condition for military traffic. Kearny's Brigade saw a little action: the Third New Jersey Volunteers skirmished with the enemy on August 29, and a day later the Second New Jersey had a brief clash, inflicting some losses on Joe Johnston's men. Patrols and reconnoitering parties went out every day, but nothing of consequence occurred.

Kearney had keyed himself for combat, and the inactivity had an adverse effect on him. He wrote long, pessimistic letters to Agnes. To him, anyone who held troops in camp instead of fighting was practically guilty of treason.

Philip did not get on with McClellan and believed that the Commanding General was disdainful of him. This feeling took seed when Kearny submitted an unsolicited strategic plan for driving the Rebels out of Virginia. He heard nothing from the General who never acknowledged having received the plan.

Kearny complained bitterly to De Peyster in a letter he wrote during September, 1861: "... In the idleness of our camps we poor generals discuss plans ... but General McClellan's policy now is to exclude everyone. At first a few generals were admitted to see him ... recently there is nobody ... This quality of reticence and secrecy may be valuable in a man of genius ... but in McClellan I consider it most unfortunate ..."

After months of training, McClellan's first offensive move, which took place in October, 1861, at Ball's Bluff, Virginia, wound up in disaster.

On November 3, 1861, venerable General Scott retired from the Army and left Washington. Old Fuss and Feathers was replaced as Commander in Chief by McClellan who also continued to head the Army of the Potomac. "I can do it all," he told Lincoln, and took the military fate of the nation in his hands.

Kearny outspokenly disapproved of this development although he was willing to give McClellan a chance. In December, 1861, he expressed his feelings in a letter to a New York friend:

To be blunt, I believe the Administration was wrong in dropping Scott... the old man's mind was as strong as ever... His high moral, military and political standing should have been preserved... Believe me, with a great admiration for Mr. Lincoln... I must say that his Administration would not survive a second Bull Run in my opinion... I am convinced McClellan feels this and is rendered overcautious by it....

I believe this is woefully wrong politically, for in the eyes of foreign governments our present inaction can only pass for pusillanimity... But Scott is gone and none more likely than McClellan remains. All are equally untried... He may yet prove us all wrong in our judgments of him....

When Kearny wrote this letter he had recently recovered from a "periodic breakdown in health." He had been subject to numerous illnesses for many years, especially after the loss of his arm.

"I live on calomel," he would remark. "I am an expert

about calomel. I've taken enough of it to kill a horse, and since I am not yet dead, I must draw the conclusion that I am stronger than a horse..."

Everyone was deceived about his physical condition because his energy overcame ailments that would have felled a man less devoted to duty. No matter how ill he might be, Philip was ready to ride when needed. Days of constant exposure and activity were too often followed by nights without sleep. During the period of his generalship Kearny aged noticeably. His hair and beard turned gray. His hawk-like face became careworn and he appeared far older than his forty-seven years. Poor health and responsibilities were not the only reasons for these physical changes. In February, 1862, while at the camp in Fairfax he received a telegram from Agnes: COME AT ONCE. ARCHIE DESPERATELY ILL WITH TYPHOID.

An aide on duty at Brigade headquarters heard Kearny cry out when the telegram was delivered. "No, dear God! Not my son!"

"I rushed to the General," the officer later said. "He was in the adjoining room standing at his field desk. I had never before seen a more desolate expression on any man's face. I asked him what was wrong. 'Lieutenant, my boy has typhoid. I must hurry home,' he said. I felt sorry for him. The General suddenly looked old and lost and hopeless. I shall never forget his anguish."

Philip set out for Bellegrove as soon as he could. The trip must have been an agonizing one. Every stop the train made was an added torture. He idolized his sturdy two-year-old son. Once, while watching her husband with Archie, Agnes had remarked: "The lad is Phil's life, and I must be grateful he still finds a place in it for me...."

As darkness fell on Wednesday, February 19, Kearny reached Bellegrove. Riding a horse he had hired in Newark, the General galloped up through a veil of freezing rain. Even before the animal stopped he vaulted off, dashed to the house, and pounded on the door.

With rain dripping from his cape, the General pushed abruptly past the servant who let him in and strode into the parlor where Agnes stood before the fire. She ran to him.

"How is he?" Kearny demanded.

"Archie is dying!" she moaned.

"I do not believe it! I will not! I dare not!" he cried and ran from the room.

"His face was chalk white ... his eyes glittered insanely," a servant remembered.

As Philip reached the top of the wide staircase his cousin, Dr. Robert Watts, met him. The General seized the doctor with his single, powerful hand. In the violence of his emotion he shook Watts, "crying out like a crazy man..."

"You must save him!" he shouted. "You will save him?" he entreated. Shoving Watts aside, he leveled a finger at him. "You *shall* save him!" It was an order, sternly delivered, as if the issue of life and death were as much in his power as the movements of his brigade.

"Phil, I'm doing my best," Watts said quietly. "Let's go downstairs.

Unable to speak, Kearny nodded and followed him to the parlor.

"Phil, who had seen so much death, who had courted it himself... slumped in a chair, motionless... gray-faced and hunched... The proud, iron-willed soldier had disappeared... Instead, I saw before me a father... crushed by imminent tragedy...." Watts said.

The excrutiating waiting lasted two days. Little Archie died on Washington's Birthday which dawned bleak, cold and rainy. Kearny was bereaved—"broken with grief," according to De Peyster who said: "... it appeared as if Phil did not greatly care to live after the death of lovely Archie...."

The General did not remain long at Bellegrove. Within a week he was with his troops again, busy with preparations for the expected spring offensive. Rumors crackled through the Army of the Potomac that McClellan was preparing to march south in a tremendous offensive.

Kearny hid his heartbreak in hard work. At times he managed to alleviate his pain, but nothing really brought him relief. "I am an empty vessel. The sky is permanently darkened for me... I shall mourn my boy forever. Yet I cannot forget that Agnes is suffering even more at home without any distraction for her sorrow... At least through duty I am afforded partial oblivion...." he confided to an aide.

Momentous events were in the making for 1862. Philip believed it would be the most crucial year in American history. "What transpires in the ensuing months will decide this nation's destiny," he said.

He differed with McClellan's concept of attacking Richmond by transporting the Army of the Potomac in ships to Fortress Monroe and then advancing up the Peninsula to the Rebel Capital. He had his own frequently expressed ideas for prosecuting the war in Virginia. De Peyster was his favorite sounding board, and early in 1862, he wrote to him from Alexandria, outlining his strategy for crushing the Rebellion:

For myself I say we should feint at Manassas, simultaneously falling on Johnston with troops from all quarters. He and all beyond him would be cut off, or get most rapidly into Manassas ... We could take and hold Winchester and then commence a turning movement cutting the Rebels from the Rappahannock; all the while offering them a pitched battle ... They would be forced to come out of their entrenchments at Manassas to get it ... We are superior to them and I do not see why we should not fight as well, and if we are beaten, then the oftener we are beaten the sooner we will learn to fight ... It is the history of all beaten people who have men and money in super abundance. ...

In 1864-65, Grant adopted this strategy—a direct advance on Richmond. The plan had to succeed, according to Kearny, "... since we enjoy command of the Chesapeake and its tributaries ... thus enabling the fleet to supply the Army as it moved onward through the various estuaries which penetrate so far as to obviate the necessity of any line of supply by land, or which at all events, by constantly affording new bases of supply, will necessitate only very short and easy wagoning transportation. ..."

But Phil was only a soldier, not a policy maker; his duty was to follow orders. This did not stop him from criticizing McClellan's plans. As late as March 4, 1862—shortly before the big push was scheduled to begin—he said: "I now proclaim distinctly... that unless a chief of proven military prestige—success under fire with troops—is put in command of the Army of the Potomac, leaving to McClellan the staff duties of General in Chief, we will come in for some awful disaster...."

On March 11, McClellan was relieved—but as General in Chief and not from his post as Commander of the Army of the Potomac. It is not difficult to imagine Kearny's reaction. Apparently the Administration did not agree that disaster was in the making, although it now realized that McClellan could not "do it all."

During the last weeks of the Army's idleness Kearny heard many complaints from local farmers that his men were raiding their henhouses and storage bins. Even more irritating to him were reports from the commanders of neighboring regiments who alleged that Phil's soldiers had looted supply dumps and made off with a mountain of equipment including blankets, clothing, knapsacks, weapons and cartridges.

These charges infuriated Kearny. He conducted an investigation which showed that some men from the Fourth New Jersey Regiment, abetted by troopers of the Lincoln Cavalry, were indeed the culprits. (The Lincolns, finally in Federal service, were encamped alongside the New Jersey Brigade.)

Kearny had the ringleaders brought before him and demanded why they had done it.

"Well, General," a spokesman for the guilty men said, "you always taught us to be prepared for anything—so we just put a few things aside against hard times."

Philip dismissed the men after delivering a "furiously profane" reprimanding. "Why, the General cussed us out for ten minutes, maybe longer, and didn't once repeat himself," an admiring private said.

The stolen equipment was returned; the pillaged food paid for out of regimental funds. The matter was closed when Kearny observed: "I now know the quickest and surest way to capture Richmond. Put a henhouse and a food bin on the far side of the city and those thieves from the Fourth New Jersey and the Lincolns will charge through hell to get at the hens and the food."

CHAPTER XVIII

EXCITED anticipation mounted daily in the New Jersey Brigade camp—in all the encampments of the Army. Everyone knew that something big was underway. Little Mac was getting set to "kick the tar out'n the Rebs." Every man was eager to "tangle" with the enemy. The Yankees remembered Bull Run and Ball's Bluff and wanted vengeance.

Probably no soldier in the Army of the Potomac awaited combat more eagerly than Kearny. He worked long hours in his headquarters, poring over reports, checking lists of supplies and equipment. When the fighting started his brigade would lack nothing if he could help it.

Philip's concern for his men was one of his outstanding traits as an officer. The high-spirited youths of the New

Jersey Brigade appreciated this and demonstrated how they felt about him one night when the General had been working late in his command post.

A group of soldiers gathered outside the Headquarters building and at a signal began to sing. They had learned Kearny's favorite songs and formed a glee club to serenade him.

The clear, strong voices rose in the darkness. They sang "Aura Lee," "Lorena," "The Harp That Once Through Tara's Halls" and other melodies. At first the General paid no attention to the singing, but soon he left his desk and went to the window. When the last song was concluded a shout arose from the shadows where hundreds of soldiers had congregated.

"Ker-nee! Ker-nee!" the men chanted.

The General stepped out into the small balcony. The men cheered as he appeared. In describing his reaction he later said:

I stood as though rooted. All those boys cheering me ... It had been my lot to prepare them for the wickedest of ordeals ... I had to turn fresh youths into soldiers ... At times I had been harsh and demanding ... to some I must have seemed a martinet. Perhaps some of them even hated me as a tyrant ... but not one of my soldiers could ever say his General had dealt unjustly with him ... I never meted out a punishment that was undeserved ... nor had I ever charged a man with wrongdoing unless possessed of irrefutable proof ... I would rather see a dozen guilty men go scot free than one innocent man wrongfully convicted ... the soldiers were my charges ... Even the worst of them merited fair treatment. If ever I had known moments of self-doubt about my abilities as a commander they would expunged by the cheers that greeted me ... I wept unashamedly before my men, and the tears ... were tears of gratitude as well as emotion. ...

The serenade concluded with a song written by one of the soldiers:

> New Jersey Blues, the bold and true,
> Though small the State, the men though few,
> Shall prove in eighteen-sixty-two.
> They'll deeds of seventy-six outdo.
> New Jersey Blues, ye bold and true,
> We're worthy Kearny, Kearny you!

Sung to the tune of "Maryland! My Maryland!" this piece was received with thunderous applause. "Perhaps the verse doesn't scan too well, but we sure liked the spirit behind the words," a sergeant of the First New Jersey observed.

A few days later Philip was leading his men against the enemy. It was no secret that McClellan had persuaded Lincoln to let him advance on Richmond by way of the Peninsula and not through Manassas. The only mystery was the exact date the campaign would be launched. However, McClellan's security arrangements were by no means watertight.

"Gambling men in Washington are betting that the first regiments will embark for Fortress Monroe on Monday, March 17," a New York journalist reported. "Men who should know better are wagging their tongues in every saloon and restaurant. A Rebel spy need do no more than take supper at Willard's and keep his ears cocked to the conversation of the highly placed officers seated about him. He will soon garner all the information Jeff Davis could want concerning the future movements of the Army of the Potomac...."

On Friday, March 7, the drummers sounded the long roll in the encampment of the New Jersey Brigade. The regiments drew up in marching order, each man with full field pack and two days' rations. The Brigade moved out at 3 P.M.

Splendidly mounted, Kearney rode at the head of the long column. Behind him came his staff; a half-dozen dashing young officers. Among them was a recent West Point graduate, yellow-haired Lieutenant George Armstrong Custer who was to achieve fame in the Civil War and lose his life almost a decade later fighting the Sioux in Montana.

The New Jersey Brigade, with troops A and H of the Lincoln Cavalry covering its flanks, had been ordered to Burke's Station on the Alexandria and Orange Railroad "for the purpose of guarding against attack by enemy irregulars, a party of laborers engaged in repairing the line." According to Kearny the men marched "elegantly" although the roads were still sloppy and muddy.

The Brigade reached Burke's at about 4 A.M. March 8, and Kearny snatched only a slight rest before he mounted again to make a personal reconnaissance of the position.

"The General had more vitality than most men half his age ... brimming with energy, he bounded onto his horse and rode off while the rest of us on the staff followed wearily in his wake ... I know not of the other staff officers, but I ached in every bone, sinew, muscle and tendon so that I could barely sit my horse," one of Kearny's aides complained.

Early Sunday, March 9, an escaped slave was brought to the brigade command tent. The young and intelligent Negro had come from Manassas with astonishing news. Joe Johnston was preparing to evacuate his bases at Manassas and Centreville. Philip was sceptical but the report was soon confirmed by other contrabands who had entered the Union lines near Burke's Station. The stories tallied exactly; the Rebels were abandoning their positions and moving south toward Richmond.

Kearny acted swiftly. Instead of awaiting definite orders he advised his Division Commander, General William B. Franklin, of what he had learned and then sent the entire New Jersey Brigade forward in a widely spread formation. A squadron of the First New York (Lincoln) Cavalry under Lieutenant Harry Hidden screened the movement. The troopers had a sharp skirmish with the Rebel rearguard at Sangster's Station, about five miles from Bull Run Creek and almost nine miles from Manassas Junction. Hidden, who had been ordered by Kearny to "move ahead cautiously and feel out the enemy's position," took a patrol of sixteen troopers and a corporal into the village of Sangster's Station in hot pursuit of fleeing Rebel pickets.

Suddenly the blue-coated horsemen were surrounded by more than a hundred Confederate infantry. Called upon to surrender, Hidden shouted to his men, "Surrender! Never! I don't relish Libby Prison! Let's cut our way out!"

"We're with you!" the troopers responded.

Yelling wildly, the Yankee cavalrymen smashed into the

encircling Rebels. The Southerners broke and fled to the surrounding woods. Hidden emerged from the trap without losing a man, and at the same time captured thirteen prisoners. Unfortunately, on the way back to the Union lines a prisoner drew a concealed pistol and fired a shot at Hidden before being cut down. The bullet struck the officer in the back, killing him instantly.

According to an eyewitness, "General Kearny had been watching the entire action through his field glasses... and when the troopers approached rode out to meet them... He arrived only moments after Lieutenant Hidden's death... although upset by the loss of the lieutenant, Kearny shook each man's hand and complimented him on his bravery...."

The following morning (Monday, March 10) elements of the First New Jersey Infantry occupied Fairfax Courthouse and pressed on to Centreville. Later the same day the rest of the Brigade swept into the abandoned fortifications at Manassas.

It was found that many of the supposed cannon which had been seen poking from the breastworks were merely "Quaker" guns—logs mounted on wheels and painted black to resemble fieldpieces. The apparently impregnable Rebel works were a fraud. Joe Johnston had completely hoodwinked McClellan.

Evidence showed that the Rebels had left Manassas in a hurry. "An immense quantity of hospital and commissary stores were found, together with eighty baggage wagons, several locomotives, five cars, two hundred tents and other valuable property; among the trophies were also seven regimental flags...." reported an officer of the Third New Jersey regiment, which had been first to enter the Rebel stronghold.

The correspondent of the New York *Herald* who had accompanied the advance described the scene for his readers:

> Smoke was still rising from the black ruins of numerous quarters and storehouses recently set afire by the retreating enemy ... Some of the quarters which had not been fired were filled with articles of value that time had not permitted their owners to carry away ... There were provisions in plentitude ... The men were not slow to appropriate what lay before them ... General Kearny was with the advance all day and gave the men free access to everything that had been left behind....
>
> As he rode into the works after their occupation and drew up in front of our lines, lifting his cap under the Stars and Stripes, three rounds of applause welcomed the hero of Churubusco and the San Antonio Gate ... All agreed that the reason for the enemy's precipitate withdrawal was the clever tactics employed by Kearny in approaching Manassas ... He had spread his brigade over the country so as to make the enemy think it to be the van of the whole Army....

In his own version of the advance to Manassas, Kearny said, "I feel that if properly supported I could have pushed the enemy even farther. My troops were the first to enter Manassas Junction. My bold Third New Jersey planted their flag and I was returning to Centreville when I met General McClellan, all his staff and some 2,000 cavalry, approaching with skirmishers out in the belief we were Rebels ... They had done the same thing at Fairfax Courthouse which I had taken some twenty-four hours earlier...."

General McClellan played down Kearny's action in seizing Manassas. In fact, he moved the Army back to its original position a few days later. When questioned as to why he did not push on, find the enemy, and force an engagement, McClellan claimed the whole Manassas affair had merely been an "elaborate maneuver" to ready his troops for the "great offensive" that was coming. He also hinted that the Rebels had learned of his plans to attack via the Peninsula route and were dropping back to defend Richmond. In his opinion Johnston's "retrograde movement" had little significance, since the real test was to come on the Peninsula.

But McClellan could not silence the criticism aimed at him. It was now clear to many that the Army of the Potomac had marked time for months, frozen into immobility by the specter of Johnston's allegedly formidable bastions. The awesome Rebel strength had turned out to be nothing more than shadows. Johnston had played a huge joke on Little Mac but no one in the North was amused.

Nathaniel Hawthorne, writing from Washington to his daughter Rose, said: "... the outcry against McClellan since the enemy's retreat from Manassas is almost universal ... Unless he achieves something wonderful ... he will be removed from command ... At least, I hope so. I never did more than half believe in him. ..." Hawthorne's prognostication did not come to pass for many months. McClellan's power still had a long course to run.

In all the North it was doubtful if anyone had more animosity toward McClellan than did Kearny. The Commander in Chief rankled Philip by—in his opinion—continuing to belittle the successes of the New Jersey Brigade from March 7-10. And he felt that McClellan had not properly acknowledged Kearny's report of the action.

"It's not for myself that I give a hoot!" Phil exploded. "I want no credit for what was accomplished. But why does he ignore the brave and loyal boys of my brigade?"

Considerations far more important than the way he felt McClellan had treated him kindled Philip's criticisms of his chief. Because Little Mac had failed to follow up the enemy after Manassas had been recaptured, Kearny was convinced that the Army of the Potomac's Commander was wrong and wrote: "The . . . truth is that instead of letting me and others push on after the panic-stricken foe and forcing him to fight a big battle and probably ending the war—for the enemy's panicky flight promised us sure success—McClellan has brought us all back. The result will be that the Rebels . . . thinking us afraid of a real stand-up fight . . . will take daring action against us . . . while we strike timidly at them. . . ."

Phil's opinion of McClellan in no way affected events. After all, he was only a brigadier general who had nothing to do with the grand strategy. Another man in Kearny's place would have kept quiet. His dissidence did him no good, but he refused to be silent.

"Nobody could muzzle Phil Kearny when he had something to get off his chest," stated O. S. "Pet" Halstead, a New Jerseyite. "Phil growled and snapped at McClellan like a peevish bulldog. Yet because he was a loyal soldier, always obeyed his orders. He carried out every command issued by his superior even though they often stuck in his craw."

Apparently McClellan appreciated Kearny's military merits despite the latter's feelings toward him. He offered the New Jersey maverick the command of General Edwin Sumner's division when that veteran was promoted to lead the Second Corps.

On learning of the offer Philip ungraciously remarked: "That's the first sound move George McClellan has made since he took over the Army of the Potomac."

Actually Kearny was delighted at the prospect of having a division, but prefaced his acceptance on the condition that his New Jersey Brigade "... which I have perfected by expending toil, zeal and effort ..." should be transferred with him. "It would be unseemly for my men to be led into battle by any other officer," he argued, proposing that the New Jersey Brigade be exchanged for one from Sumner's division.

"I can understand your sentiments, General Kearny," McClellan replied. "However, I shall leave the whole matter up to General Franklin. After all, this concerns his division. If he agrees to make the swap, I shall approve it."

Grudgingly, Kearny had to admit: "McClellan has a decent streak; at least he sees how I feel about my Brigade." Having received encouragement from the Commanding General, Kearny shopped around in Sumner's division until he found a brigadier general willing to switch over to Franklin.

"It was Franklin who soured my hopes," Kearny grumbled, "for he refused to part with the New Jersey Brigade."

Franklin's reason for turning down the proposition was a practical one. "Why should I surrender such a fine body of troops? I will not exchange the New Jersey Brigade for one that might not be its equal. I don't usually buy a pig in a poke and I won't do so now," Franklin snapped during a meeting with Kearny at Division Headquarters.

"Then I have no alternative, General," Kearny said. "I will remain with my men."

"What? You're not going to take the division?" Franklin cried.

"No, sir."

"I can't believe it. Do you realize what this means, Kearny? You're turning down a second star!"

"General Franklin, those boys mean more to me than any promotion. I shall advise General McClellan to seek another candidate for Sumner's division. If you are through with me, sir, I must return to my unit."

"Yes, yes, you may go," Franklin said. Long after Kearny had left the division commander stared into space and kept repeating, "He turned down a star. I don't see it. He turned down a star."

The news soon spread that Kearny had chosen to remain with his brigade rather than accept a division. When word reached the brigade encampment hundreds of men drifted to headquarters and awaited his return.

At last he came riding up, followed by two aides. A shattering cheer greeted him as the men surged forward. "Ker-nee! Ker-nee!" they roared. The exuberant soldiers clung to his stirrups and bridle; they reached up to touch him and surged about so thickly that he could not pass through the crowd. After awhile the provost marshal's guards cleared a way to the Headquarters building where Kearny dismounted. He made a brief speech from the porch.

"My destiny is linked to yours..." he told them. "We shall be invincible during the trials ahead. You will not fail me, as I have not failed you! Soon... our... Army will be locked in battle... and when the test comes let it be said of the New Jersey Brigade that no man faltered...."

Another demonstration erupted after the speech and lasted over an hour. The brigade band appeared and the soldiers fell into line behind it. Regimental and company color-bearers took their places and soon a full review was under way. Company after company paraded past Kearny, the men cheering him as they marched by. He acknowledged the tribute by doffing his cap.

"I'll never forget the General standing there, so straight and fine looking, with his French cap raised. It gave me a shiver of pride just to see him," said a young soldier.

The next day a committee of enlisted men called on Philip. They had been sent "on behalf of the entire brigade to advise the General" that his soldiers appreciated what he had done. "What we really want to say, sir," the group's spokesman blurted out, "is that we'd follow you through the gates of Hell!"

CHAPTER XIX

PHILIP Kearny always resented being subordinate to men of lesser military experience. After his refusal to take Sumner's division Kearny wondered whether he would be given another chance at a promotion.

He continued to be annoyed with what he considered "useless" orders coming from men he labeled "my inferior superiors." Philip had absolute confidence in his own ability to accomplish anything.

"I can do a better job at division, corps or even army level than any man now holding higher rank than mine," he stated flatly to a senior aide with whom he had served in Mexico. "Why do they not recognize my qualifications for important command?"

Perhaps the aide had grown tired of Phil's frequent complaint that he was being discriminated against. He said, "I may be presuming on our long acquaintance, but I must respectfully point out to the General that he could even now be in command of a division had he not refused it—"

"You know why I did that! I wanted to take this brigade with me," Kearny interrupted.

"Yes, sir. But it's a fact that a man can't both keep his cake and eat it," the aide replied.

Apparently the remark had some effect; after that Philip seldom complained about his status in the Army. He also made it clear that he would not again "... allow sentiment to guide me ... I am not indispensable to the New Jersey Brigade ... perhaps it is my immodesty which forces me to believe that may be the case," he wrote a relative.

On March 26, 1862, he received proof that his efforts were appreciated. The New Jersey Legislature passed a resolution which declared:

Resolved: That New Jersey highly appreciates the fidelity of General Philip Kearny in declining proffered promotion rather than separate himself from the command of the Jerseymen entrusted to him. . . .

A few days later the same body unanimously approved a second resolution which stated in part:

Resolved: That having already testified our high appreciation of the self-sacrifice and fidelity to his trust which led General Kearny to decline promotion rather than to leave his brigade, we now express our regret at the existence of any such necessity and respectfully suggest to those in authority ... the propriety of combining all the New Jersey troops on the Potomac into one division ... under the command of General Kearny, whose devotion for his soldiers, care for their comfort and discipline, and brilliant qualities as an officer entitle the country to his services in a higher position than the one he now occupies.

Copies were sent to the Secretary of War, but nothing came of the idea to form a New Jersey division. Kearny believed that volunteer regiments would fight better if they were formed into divisions by states. The concept was not approved by the War Department where objections to it were raised on the grounds that state pride might cause dissension among the troops and no units higher than brigades contained men exclusively from the same state.

The flowery resolutions of the New Jersey Legislature were soon buried under the avalanche of dispatches and communiqués pouring into the War Department from the Army of the Potomac as McClellan's highly touted Peninsular Campaign began.

His troops climbed aboard an astounding conglomeration of ships which ranged from big steamers to New York ferryboats that had once shuttled across the East River from Brooklyn to Manhattan. Great convoys propelled by sail and steam churned down the coast to Fortress Monroe on the tip of the Peninsula. The Army of the Potomac was soon to get its first trial under McClellan, and the nation looked on confidently.

"Now the Johnny Rebs are in for a thrashing," was the consensus of Northern opinion. Surely nothing on earth could stop Little Mac who was heading south with the "strongest army ever gathered on the North American continent, or for that matter anywhere in the world," wrote a

New York *Herald* reporter as he watched the regiments embarking at Alexandria.

Kearny's men waited impatiently at their camp in Alexandria; every piece of equipment was packed and the outfit stood ready to move at a moment's notice. Any hour, any minute, orders were expected to move them down-river and aboard a transport. "The embarkment of the Army had commenced on March 17," noted a member of Kearny's staff, "and we daily anticipated the word to move out. Neighboring brigades and regiments received such orders and went off while we sat like despondent and neglected waifs...."

Then on April 5, a dispatch rider sped up to the New Jersey Brigade's headquarters with a message for Kearny. The brigade was to advance overland along the Alexandria and Orange Railroad to Catlett's Station on the way to Richmond and there await further instructions.

Philip read the orders with unrestrained joy. "Brilliant! Elegant!" he cried. "They've seen the light!" He believed that McClellan meant to execute a gigantic pincers movement, pressing the Rebel Capital by way of Manassas and pushing down the Peninsula at the same time.

The brigade left camp "... with bands playing, flags flying and spirits high...." It made a route march to Catlett's Station and went into bivouac. Three days passed without word from the High Command. "General Kearny dashed back and forth inspecting the outposts, just to keep himself busy ... When not in the saddle he could be seen pacing outside his comand tent ... his former good humor evaporated... and dark frowns replaced his smiles...." the Brigade Chief of Staff noted.

Orders which evoked a "torrent of oaths from Kearny" were finally received. The brigade was instructed to "return to camp in Alexandria... there to board a transport for conveyance to Yorktown...." Kearny obeyed his orders but in such a fury that a soldier recalled, "We marched back to Alexandria... with the General riding up front ... he set a pace that forced the poor fellows in the rear to trot to keep up with the column... General Phil must've been madder than a hornet... because they'd recalled us when he thought we'd high-tail it right into Richmond...."

At Alexandria, General Franklin advised Kearny to hold his men in readiness; they were scheduled to embark the following day (April 10). But something went wrong with the arrangements and the Jersey troops had to wait a week before going up a gangplank. During the interlude Phil tried to find out why he had been pulled back from Catlett's, but could learn nothing more enlightening than that "General McClellan changed his mind."

The waiting time passed slowly, and Kearny's hair-trigger temper erupted on several occasions. According to a member of his staff "... the General was in a constant pet... he felt slighted because the brigade embarkation had been postponed... He grew fretful and snappish, for all the world like a willful child... Yet, I knew his ill humor concealed the deep concern he felt for the future of his men. He told me, 'If the buffoons above us cannot carry off a simple movement of troops without blundering... My God, what will they do to us in combat?' "

He was so disgusted with the poorly organized transport system that he wrote Agnes: "... this expedition, which I believe to have been conceived in weakness, is a cripple at birth... Thus misbegotten, its lot can only be misfortune... its ending, humiliation...."

The black moods brought on by "bungling, botching and boobery" caused Kearny many unpleasant hours. Still mourning Archie, he sat alone in his tent, "... grieving in silence... He was as a wounded lion... mighty and majestic, even at his most vulnerable moment...." was the way his Chief of Staff described him.

Those who knew Philip best were used to his volatile behavior. "He could soar from despondency to exuberance with the swiftness of a hawk...." a friend had said of him. This was demonstrated on Wednesday, April 16, when he was summoned to General Franklin's headquarters. "Kearny rode away with wrath and gloom on his brow... he returned smiling in the April sunshine...." an officer observed.

Kearny's euphoria was the result of what he had learned at division. The New Jersey Brigade was definitely scheduled to embark Thursday, April 17. "I have seen the steamer with my own eyes. She is called *Elm City* and a finer ship could not be found... We shall soon be at grips with the foe...." he wrote Agnes that night.

However, Kearny did not tell his wife the real reason for his cheerfulness. He did reveal it to his staff. According to plans, the brigade was to sail for Yorktown on the *Elm City* and two smaller vessels. On reaching the York River they were to force a landing with the support of a gunboat flotilla.

"Think of it, gentlemen! We shall be in the thick of the fighting from the very outset. Our colors shall be in the van! Is that not a brilliant prospect?" Kearny beamed.

The promise of early combat had transformed him. "Seldom have I seen him in such animated spirits," said the Commander of a neighboring brigade. "One might have thought Phil was anticipating a party rather than a deadly struggle."

Phil's freshly acquired good humor saved Private Henry Bingham, Company A, First New Jersey Volunteers, from serious punishment. The soldier was on sentry duty in a remote sector. Instead of standing to his post as ordered, Bingham unbuttoned his blouse, sat down under a tree, and became engrossed in a "penny-dreadful" novel. He felt perfectly safe in doing this: the sergeant of the guard was not due on his rounds for at least an hour, and Bingham was almost certain that no one else would bother to check that isolated post. There surely was no danger from the enemy; the nearest Southern soldier was some forty miles away.

Suddenly Bingham heard horses. He leaped up. The book fell to the ground at his feet, and he had no time to button his blouse or grab his rifle. He saw General Kearny and "a flock of shoulder straps" coming straight at him. The General had decided to check the guard posts himself.

Terror-stricken, Bingham stared at Kearny. "I figured I was a gonner for sure... I knew how rough General Phil could get... I like to bust out bawling right there, I was so scared and sorry for myself...." Bingham wrote his parents.

In his version of what happened next: "General Phil leaned down from his horse and pierced me with his cold eyes... he stared hard and long... then all of a sudden he smiled... 'Soldier,' he says, 'you were malingering on guard duty. Another time, I'd have you properly bucked and gagged... but this is a special day... I've just learned we'll soon be in combat. How does that strike you?'... 'Oh, fine, sir! That's a big thing,' I says, trying to act all het up. 'You have the spirit, lad! Next time be more careful and attend to your duty!' he says... and General Phil and the shoulder straps were gone in a cloud of dust, and my heart was thumping like an old bass drum...."

On April 17, without any further delays, the brigade marched to the Alexandria boat landings and boarded the transports. Kearny had been assigned luxurious quarters, but was distressed by the miserable, cramped living space in the troop area below. He apologized to his men and explained they would have to put up with the inconvenience for only a short time.

Escorted by a gunboat flotilla, the *Elm City* and the other ships weighed anchor and moved slowly down river to the open water. The convoy inched along with frequent stops for unknown reasons. It took six days to reach the mouth of the York River where Kearny still believed he was to make an assault landing. At the moment he was not aware that the big attack on Yorktown had already bogged into siege operations. McClellan had decided not to risk a frontal assault.

He believed Yorktown to be strongly fortified and heavily manned—an impression gained from his scouts who had seen "hundreds of Rebels marching into Yorktown." Had McClellan dared to press hard, he would have learned that the enemy under General John Magruder numbered only about 13,000, and that Union scouts had been deceived by Magruder's clever ruse of marching and countermarching the same men to make them seem like a huge force. In addition, the weather turned rainy, compounding the Young Napoleon's problems. He used the bad weather as an excuse for not attacking and advised the War Department that his artillery was mired in Virginia mud.

When the *Elm City* hove to at the mouth of the York River (April 23) the Army was stalled outside the Rebel works. Instead of loading into longboats and charging ashore, the New Jersey Brigade sat in its transports to await developments. When he saw what had happened, Kearny again flew into a rage. "They keep my boys cooped up in these pigsty ships where they'll sicken and die for sure; yet they dare not risk sending them against the enemy... It is sheer idiocy!" he ranted to his staff.

The Brigade lingered on shipboard until April 30, and then went ashore to join the remainder of Franklin's Division. That day as Kearny stood by the water's edge supervising the landing of his men a messenger delivered a dispatch. He read it and showed the paper to an aide. The message was:

Special Order #129:

       HEADQUARTERS
       ARMY OF THE POTOMAC
       30 April, 1862

B. G. Philip Kearny, commanding 1st N.J. Brigade relieved of that duty, effective 2 May and assigned to command 3rd Division, IIIrd Corps, in place of General C. S. Hamilton, relieved.

       H. C. WILLIAMS
       COLONEL, U.S.A.
       A.A.G.

"Sir, this is wonderful news! Congratulations!" the aide cried.

"You understand, Captain, I cannot again refuse a promotion. Please assemble the brigade when all units have landed. I want to speak to them," Kearny said huskily.

Later that day the First New Jersey Brigade, drawn up in parade formation, was addressed by Philip for the last time.

"Gallant soldiers ... I must say good-bye ... Carry your colors high in battle and with pride ... You are well trained, well disciplined ... steeled for combat ... It has been my privilege to command you ... I shall never forget my Jersey boys ... And now ... Good luck!"

He rode slowly away, along the line of troops. The men did not cheer; they stood stiffly at attention. "Even the stoniest sergeant's eyes filled with tears when General Phil went past ... I felt heavy hearted to see him leave, but glad that he was getting a higher rank which he so well deserved...." a private wrote home.

After the sad leave-taking Kearny joined his new command. As a Division Commander under General Samuel Heintzelman, he led three brigades made up of troops from New York, Pennsylvania, Maine and Michigan. The Third Corps was divided into two divisions—Kearny's and Hooker's. "Fighting Joe" Hooker held the sector to the left of Kearny before Yorktown.

CHAPTER XX

When Kearny took over the division, final preparations had been made to assault Yorktown. McClellan had brought up his heavy siege guns. The cannon were dragged into place through mud so deep that one officer claimed he saw a mule sink out of sight on what was supposed to be a main road. "It was only a small mule, though," he said, to modify his statement.

The big push on Yorktown was to be made on May 4, but Joe Johnston again outwitted McClellan by ordering General John Magruder to evacuate on the night of May 3. As at Manassas, McClellan had been held up by a foe far inferior in numbers and equipment. Magruder's little army had delayed the Army of the Potomac an entire month because McClellan had feared to risk an all-out attack with forces large enough to have overwhelmed Magruder—90,000 infantry, 10,000 cavalry, 50 artillery batteries and a siege train of 100 guns.

Thus on May 4, instead of moving in under the bombardment of cannon, one of Kearny's brigade commanders, General Charles Jameson, advanced cautiously through empty Rebel entrenchments and entered Yorktown. "No one but McClellan could have hesitated to attack us," Johnston later told Robert E. Lee.

McClellan informed his troops that they had scored a "shattering victory," and went in pursuit of the retreating Rebels. Screened by General George Stoneman's cavalry, Heintzelman's corps was sent after Johnston. "Fighting Joe" Hooker's division had been picked to lead the chase, while Kearny—to his disgust—was left in the rearmost position, separated from Hooker by Sumner's 30,000-man Second Corps.

Sunday, May 4, dawned hot, clear and dusty; a remarkable change from the preceding days of steady rainfall. The temperature rose so rapidly that Hooker's men flung off all superfluous baggage, and a number were stricken by heat. The relentless race went on. By midafternoon Stoneman's troopers caught up with the enemy, and skirmishing flared near the Whittaker House a few miles north of Williamsburg.

Hooker soon tangled with the Confederate rear guard in a spirited action. Only one of Sumner's brigades joined the fighting, which broke off at dark. That night the rain started again; a miserable drizzle at first and then a steady downpour.

On Monday, May 5, it was still raining as a dispatch

rider sloshed through the mud with a message from Hooker to Kearny. "Come with all haste . . . I am hard pressed," the note read.

"Tell Hooker I'm on the way," Phil advised the courier.

As Kearny prepared for battle he heard the sounds of conflict up ahead. That morning his men learned the kind of general they now had. Kearny did not know why Hooker had failed to call for help from Sumner who was close by, but did not question the request. Hooker was in a jam. "I determined to do my best to extricate him from it," Philip wrote later.

The Third Division, Third Corps, pushed up a muddy road clogged with mired baggage wagons. The division was having a hard time getting by the vehicles when Kearny came racing to the front of his columns. He rose in his stirrups and shook his fist at the men guarding the baggage train.

"Tip those wagons out of my way! I've been ordered up to fight! I'll permit no wagons to hamper me!" he roared.

When an officer of the guard remonstrated that he could not move the vans because they were stuck in the mud Kearney bellowed, "Move them, I say! Or I'll put the torch to them!"

Somehow the roadway was cleared without resorting to arson, and the Third Division waded forward. Kearny's men passed open fields where numbers of Union troops were unaccountably standing idle, although the battle had grown more intense.

He prodded his brigades until they reached the battle

front. Quickly forming the men into a line of battle, Phil tried to ascertain the situation. All seemed confusion; nobody quite knew what was going on. Some units were fighting in the open, others in woods and thickets, stumbling about in the murky rain. At one place Kearny came upon a company of Michigan men from his Third Brigade. Instead of shooting, the men were huddled in a bunch under the dripping trees.

"What's this? Why aren't you in action?" he demanded in a terrible voice.

"Sir, we don't know where the enemy is!" an officer said.

"You don't know! Then, find out! Here, I'll show you!" With that Kearny spurred across the field to a copse about a hundred yards away. Instantly, rifles crackled at him from one end of the woods to the other. Bullets kicked up spurts of mud all around, but he raced back unharmed.

"There!" he shouted pointing. "There's the target! Now go in and kick those rebels out!"

Hooker's exhausted men perked up as the reinforcements arrived. "It's Kearny! It's Kearny!" they yelled to one another.

A captain in the Excelsior Brigade of Hooker's division wrote: "I saw Kearny come on the field . . . and of course had heard what a fierce fighter he was . . . but in all my days I never witnessed anything to equal what I saw him do . . . He rode in front of the enemy's lines, exposing himself so the Rebels would uncover their position . . ."

During the battle Kearny remained at the front almost constantly. He knew that many of his troops were under fire for the first time. "It was incumbent upon me to inspire those men ... I did whatever I could, visiting each regiment engaging the enemy...." he said later.

That day every soldier in the division saw Phil at least once, dashing across the battle line, standing in his stirrups, kepi on his sword tip, reins in his teeth—his staff officers close behind him. Somehow the knowledge that his General was running the same risks made a green private feel better. It was reassuring to know that the General "gave a hoot and holler about what was happening to us," one Pennsylvanian put it.

The fighting at Williamsburg raged all day in the driving rain. Those who had marched into battle as raw soldiers left it regarding themselves as veterans. They had "seen the elephant" and were mighty proud of it. Kearny was quick to praise his men, even while bullets were still flying.

"Good boys! That was elegant!" he called out to the Fortieth New York Volunteers as the regiment captured a Rebel position at bayonet point.

Phil was where no general should have been during action—in the front rank of the attackers. The New Yorkers appreciated what he had done, but General Heintzelman, his Corps Commander, cried in apoplectic anger, "Doesn't Kearny realize he's a general? A *general*, not a reckless shavetail to lead a bayonet charge!"

At last the shooting died down. Johnston had not meant it to be more than a rear-guard action; he had never intended to make an all-out stand at Williamsburg. Under cover of darkness he drew back toward Richmond in the rain.

The Army of the Potomac had fought its first big battle and had done well, even though mistakes were made. Sumner, for example, had not put more than one brigade of his 30,000 troops into the battle line, but stood aside waiting for orders that never came.

The men were tired yet they rallied to cheer McClellan when he came up from the rear, his once natty uniform soggy and mud splattered. Regiment after regiment applauded him as he pounded across the sodden fields on his way to the front.

If anything, Kearny's dislike of McClellan deepened after Williamsburg. The Commander in Chief had arrived at the firing line as the battle was ending, in time to watch a spirited charge by General Winfield Scott Hancock's brigade—the closing bit of action of the day. Because of this, McClellan believed that Hancock had done most of the fighting. In his first dispatch to Secretary of War Stanton he had said: "Hancock was superb..." and made no mention of Hooker's or Kearny's contributions.

Philip was furious when he learned of this. "What must I do to get justice at his hands?" he cried.

Actually McClellan's mistake was an honest one and he subsequently admitted it in a dispatch which fully credited the achievements of his two temperamental generals. A week after the battle McClellan wrote Stanton:

... I wish to bear testimony to the splendid conduct of Hooker's and Kearny's divisions of Heintzelman's corps. Hooker for seven hours gallantly withstood the attacks of greatly superior forces ... Kearny arrived in time to restore the fortunes of the day.

If I had had the full information I now have in regard to the troops above named when I first telegraphed they would then have been specially mentioned and commended... I spoke only of what I knew at the time and I am pleased to now give full credit to all concerned....

This was a major admission for McClellan to have made, but it was wasted effort as far as two of his officers were concerned.

"The so-called Young Napoleon had no choice but to correct himself," Kearny sneered. "Everyone knows how Hooker and I saved the Army," he told friends, with his characteristic immodesty.

And nothing McClellan could do or say would satisfy Hooker. He hated the Commanding General with such intensity that someone remarked, "Joe detests Little Mac worse than a kid hates sulphur and molasses... and for the same reasons... He cannot abide sight, taste or smell of McClellan...."

Williamsburg enhanced Philip's already glittering reputation as a fighter. He had set a splendid example for the men of his division. "General Phil doesn't know fear... The way he stands up when the bullets are flying... somehow, seeing him on the firing line bolsters even the most craven heart...." a New York soldier said.

In his own version of Williamsburg, Kearny made this summation:

When I arrived on the field everything was confused... Men huddled in masses, artillery was bogged in mud, infantry straggled and waded through the woods... the cavalry, baggage wagons and all sorts of vehicles inched along miry roads... Panic would have been ruin... I knew most of the troops had never been under fire... Any enemy success would be certain to stir up a panic in our ranks. This I resolved to prevent... It is true that at times I was fearfully exposed and have been accused by some as having behaved in a reckless manner... but I could not do otherwise... my poor shaken men had to be shown how to behave like soldiers... and they responded in brilliant style....

Stories about Phil began to circulate—tales that contained the stuff of legends. A Rebel prisoner allegedly said, "Who's that one-armed officer? He's got a charmed life. We've been plugging at him all day and never came close. That's the luckiest man in the world! And what a soldier! What a soldier!"

When his men came up to the firing line Kearny noticed some of them nervously ducking as shots whistled by. He galloped to them and shouted, "Don't flinch, boys! They're shooting at me, not at you! I know that!"

"Sure, General, you know it and we know it, but do the Rebs know it?" a private asked.

Laughter rippled along the ranks, and the tension was broken. "That's it, boys! That's it! Go in gaily!" Kearny cried. With a flourish of his kepi he galloped off, bullets kicking up dirt at his horse's heels. The scared rookies forgot their fears and went into the fight "gaily."

The Army had its favorite yarn about Kearny and it was retold around countless campfires. A planter's house near Williamsburg had been occupied by a brigade headquarters staff of the Third Division. Just as the place was being taken over Kearny happened to come along. In the parlor an officer found a decanter of whisky which he offered around, but everyone refused a drink fearful that the liquor had been poisoned and purposely left behind by the enemy. Kearny listened to the apprehensive talk for a moment, grabbed the bottle, poured himself a stiff drink and downed it.

"If I'm not dead in fifteen minutes, take all of the whisky you want. Now get to work!" he snapped, stomping out to his horse and galloping away, the brigade staff gaping after him.

CHAPTER XXI

AFTER the Battle of Williamsburg, McClellan advanced his army down the Peninsula with such caution that Kearny called him "the Virginia Creeper." "We advance, not as fierce invaders, but like timid trespassers. I know not what the Young Napoleon has in mind... assuredly he can not hope to capture Richmond by our present actions... The hour calls for audacity... instead we are offered timorousness...." he grumbled in a letter to Agnes.

With no major resistance to bar its way the Army of the Potomac covered only slightly better than fifty miles in a period of three weeks. "Even a snail eventually arrives at his destination...." wrote a disgruntled officer during the last week in May when the Army at last debouched in the dank and swampy marshlands on the north bank of the Chickahominy River near Richmond.

Some Yankee troops were so close to the Rebel Capital that they could see the city's spires. Heintzelman's forward posts were Richmond's outskirts. "My men can hear the bells of St. Paul's . . . If only the Young Napoleon gathered his nerve and loosed one tremendous blow . . . I can promise that we would take Richmond at our ease," Philip informed a New York friend.

But no such blow was ever delivered. Instead McClellan wasted the days in sending telegrams to Washington demanding more troops, before daring to risk an offensive. His relations with the Government grew worse.

As usual, Kearny made no effort to hide his personal feelings. No one to whom he complained about McClellan—and they were not few—took his words at face value; by this time everybody knew his penchant for letting off steam.

However, many did seriously doubt the Commander in Chief and McClellan did little to allay their suspicions or to alleviate the misunderstandings which alienated him from Government officials. Even Stanton, once a close friend, now looked upon him with misgivings. The Abolitionists openly accused him of an overly solicitous concern for Southern property and the returning of runaway slaves who entered his lines.

McClellan, in turn, grew increasingly difficult. He imagined that everyone connected with the Government was in an insidious plot to blacken his name and overthrow him. Even his most steadfast supporter, President Lincoln, did not escape Little Mac's virulence. When Lincoln urged him to break the enemy's lines the General confided to a trusted aide: "I am strongly tempted to reply that he had better come down here and do it himself."

"I am hounded by the Rebels on one side and the Abolitionists and other scoundrels on the other," McClellan said. Beset as he was, he well knew that a victory at Richmond would silence the derogatory talk. He wanted desperately to win, but believed that the enemy outnumbered his own forces. He had reached this conclusion on the basis of reports submitted by Allan Pinkerton of the famous Pinkerton National Detective Service which served as a Union spy organization.

According to Pinkerton's estimates the Rebels had nearly 200,000 men defending Richmond. Even the remote possibility that the report had any worth was sufficient to keep McClellan from making a bold move. The actual facts were that he had double the troops Johnston could muster.

To Kearny, within earshot of Richmond's church bells, the situation was galling. His impatience with McClellan was amplified daily as no decisive action was taken. Philip felt certain that Johnston would break the stalemate unless McClellan moved first.

Little Mac did extend one wing of the Army by moving some divisions across to the south bank of the Chickahominy so that his forces now straddled the stream. Kearny thought the move a blunder. "If the river should rise, we'd be in a pretty fix," he pointed out.

Philip was not optimistic about a Union success if a battle were joined. On May 28, he predicted: "... The General has been too slow; he should have annihilated the enemy at Williamsburg before they reached the Chickahominy. I believe we will soon be locked in a deadly struggle ... perhaps it will break a few hours from now ... If a Bull Run should ensue I expect that my division will be the only one to escape intact. I have my men completely in hand ... and have prepared for all exigencies...."

The battle which Kearny had foreseen was not long in coming. During the afternoon of Wednesday, May 30, a rainstorm broke in the vicinity of Richmond. This unusually rainy month had produced some heavy downpours but nothing to equal this cloudburst. The rain fell in torrents; the sluggish Chickahominy turned into a wild and raging flood whose churning waters swept away the Union pontoon bridges and made the fords impassable, thus isolating the troops McClellan had sent to the south side of the river.

The night of the 30th, the storm grew worse. Lightning blasted the sky—not in flashes, but with "sheets of flame which enveloped whole bivouacs in an eerie glare," said an officer in the Excelsior Brigade of Hooker's Division. The same man described bolts of "electric fire" running along the lines of stacked rifles, "tipping the points of the bayonets with flame, like jets of gas."

Joe Johnston, who had retreated all the way from Yorktown before McClellan's ponderous march, saw his moment to strike back. The Union Fourth Corps was cut off from the main body of the Yankee Army by the flooded Chickahominy. On Thursday, May 31, as the rain clouds were dispelled by a strong breeze and the sun broke forth Johnston made a surprise attack with Daniel H. Hill's division against General Silas Casey of Keyes' corps at a place called Seven Pines, or Fair Oaks. Casey, whose men had not finished digging in, was so surprised that a new expression "Come Casey" spread throughout the Army of the Potomac. It meant to be taken wholly unawares.

The startled Yankees fought back hard, but Hill's tough veterans charged out of the dripping woods and completely routed Casey's hapless division. The Rebels soon outflanked him and then threw James Longstreet's and G. W. Smith's divisions into the onslaught. For awhile it seemed as though the Yankees would be cut to ribbons, especially when General Darius Couch's division, also of Keyes' Corps, suffered the same fate as Casey's troops. The Union forces south of the Chickahominy faced imminent disaster.

But just as at Williamsburg, up came Kearny to stop the enemy for a vital two-and-one-half hours. At times his lines bent and almost broke, but inspired by their fiery General, Kearny's men slugged it out with Hill, Longstreet and Smith, trading blow for blow.

At one crucial point the Rebels captured two guns of a Union battery. Kearny sped to an infantry company and raising high his single arm, shouted, "Help me get those guns, boys! I'd give my other arm for them!"

"Keep your arm, General!" a soldier yelled. "We'll take those guns!"

With Kearny leading, the soldiers retook the cannon with their bayonets. The battle of Seven Pines was a confused melee. "It was more like a Five Points' brawl than a military engagement," opined a New York participant. Fighting flared everywhere at once without method or order. Men died in flooded swampland and on the muddy river banks; wounded soldiers crept into the tangled underbrush to perish unseen. Artillery pieces sank in the boggy earth; horses floundered to their hocks in mud. No one knew the precise situation at any time. Field commanders could not judge what was happening a hundred yards away.

When the Colonel of a Michigan regiment reported to Kearny for orders he asked, "Shall I take my men in through the clearing or through the woods?"

"Oh, go in anywhere, Colonel, go in anywhere. You'll find lovely fighting all along the line," Kearny answered.

Later Union General Sumner, whose men called him The Bull because of his deep voice, got his Second Corps over the swirling river on a makeshift bridge, and drove it into the fray with a spirit he had not shown at Williamsburg. Other Northern units splashed and struggled through the wild water and plugged the gaps in the line.

Halted by Kearny and then driven back by Union fire power, the Confederates slowly gave ground. As the battle was ending a Yankee sharpshooter hit General Joe Johnston in the shoulder. Then a shell splinter pierced his chest and he was carried to the rear, badly wounded. Robert E. Lee succeeded to the command and the Army of Northern Virginia found its true leader.

Seven Pines ended indecisively. Neither side gained any ground; the armies held the identical positions they had occupied before the shooting. But with one great difference: some 12,000 men—Yankee and Confederate—were numbered as killed, wounded or missing.

Compared with Seven Pines, Williamsburg had been a mere skirmish; the Army of the Potomac was no longer

McClellan's showpiece. Spruce uniforms were ragged and dirty; the young men had aged. Instead of fresh-faced boys, they were bearded, hard-eyed veterans.

Phil Kearny, who had spent a lifetime with soldiers, rode through his division's bivouac after the battle. He looked his troops over and said, "... my men have been tempered in battle ... now the youthful dreams of bold deeds and reckless adventure have faded away ... They have beheld the depths of Hell and nothing will ever again be the same for any of them ... You cannot expect young men—boys really—to undergo the rigors of war without a price being paid ... and that price is the innocence and sweetness of youth. War corrupts those it touches ... it twists and distorts lives ... it blights youth ... and that is the real awfulness of it ... not the killing, the carnage, the destruction ... War is horrible because it strangles youth...."

CHAPTER XXII

FOLLOWING the fighting at Seven Pines a lull fell across the battle front. The men dug in along the Chickahominy and in the unhealthy miasmas of the swamps there many sickened with fever. Day after day passed without action. Sometimes a fire fight broke out between the picket posts, but on the whole the bright Virginia June went by unmarred by any great activity.

Realizing that this idleness was not good for his men, Philip hit upon a spirit-lifting idea. He secured bolts of red flannel and had the cloth cut into small diamond-shaped patches. He distributed these bits of cloth to every man in his troops. Officers were ordered to wear the patch on the left side of their caps; enlisted men on the crown. "Now you are marked men," Kearny told his division.

"The enemy will quail when he sees that scarlet patch, and well he may! In the attack you have always driven him; when assailed you have always repulsed him!"

The soldiers took to the device eagerly and it quickly became known as the Kearny Patch. They wore it proudly, to the envy of other outfits. This identifying insignia was the first of its kind in the Army. (The Kearny Patch was the forerunner of the modern division patch.) Similar emblems were eventually adopted throughout the Union Army at a later date and each unit had its own distinctive mark.

Kearny had devised the patch for other than morale-boosting reasons. During the welter of the fighting at Seven Pines he had noticed the difficulty of telling various organizations apart. Amid the confusion of battle soldiers often became separated from their companies; companies were isolated from their regiments and wandered aimlessly about. This could not happen again in Kearny's Division; one glance at the scarlet patch on a man's cap would tell where he belonged.

The respite on the Chickahominy was rudely broken during the night of June 13–14 when an alarm was raised that Rebel cavalry was on the loose behind the lines. The Confederate thunderbolt, Jeb Stuart, had slashed through the Army of the Potomac's outposts with a thousand horsemen in a sweeping raid that carried him completely around the Army's positions in one of the most daring of cavalry strokes.

Few in the Army of the Potomac slept that night. Cavalry squadrons rode helter-skelter in the darkness. Contradictory reports had Stuart in a dozen places at once. Picket posts were trebled and skittery sentries fired at anything that moved. "It was a bad night for cows," a private wrote. "We shot two in front of our position, thinking they were Rebs in the woods."

Brigades double-timed back and forth. The long roll sounded steadily, and buglers blew "To Arms!" until they were exhausted. But no one caught up with Jeb Stuart. He outsmarted, outrode and outfought McClellan's whole army. His men cut telegraph lines, tore up railroad tracks, and burned stores of supplies. The Union rear was disrupted and paralyzed. Having achieved his purpose, Stuart slipped away safely. Kearny gave the Rebel raider's feat the highest praise he could bestow on any man—friend or enemy. "Stuart is a veritable *Chasseur d'Afrique!*" he glowingly exclaimed.

After Stuart's coup McClellan grew even warier. He worried about details and busied himself with trifles, yet still created the impression that he was about to undertake a decisive step. "Everything is in readiness to attack," he assured Stanton. "I shall move as soon as the weather and the ground permit."

Work details toiled to improve roads; engineers threw bridges across the Chickahominy; regiment after regiment advanced to the south side of the river. The men faced expectantly toward Richmond. The sun was shining; the swampy land dried out so that even isolated wagon trails could carry the weight of heavy siege guns which rolled ponderously toward the front. The troops awaited the word to march. The time seemed right for the "big thing."

McClellan inched closer to Richmond every day, hauling up the giant siege guns he had expected to use against Johnston at Yorktown. He threw up earthworks all along the front to protect his positions, confident that his plan could not fail. First a shattering barrage to blast the foe; then an overpowering assault along the whole line. Soon Richmond would be his, McClellan kept reassuring the War Department.

He could not know that General Lee had already deduced his strategy. It was a sound concept, and Lee frankly admitted that he could not withstand an artillery pounding followed by an overwhelming infantry onslaught. He was not willing to "consent to such a program," and took countermeasures. He shrewdly noticed that McClellan had left General Fitz-John Porter's Fifth Corps on the north side of the Chickahominy while the main Yankee strength was being massed on the south bank.

Thus, while McClellan was writing that he would be "making history the day after tomorrow" Lee made history of his own. He decided that Porter's corps was the Yankee's weak spot and prepared for a blow at that point.

As Lee was planning his riposte Kearny expressed a few ideas on the military situation. On June 22, in a letter to Agnes, whom he had not seen for months, Philip made a remarkably prophetic prediction:

> I am sorry I cannot give you interesting news. Here we are at deadlock again. Manassas over again—both parties entrenched up to the eyes; both waiting for something to occur... It only

required McClellan to put forth...his military might and Richmond would have been ours. But no; delay upon delay; fortifications as if we were beaten, met by stronger fortifications...supineness in our camps, met by daring forays by them; the boasted influence of our reserve artillery counterbalanced by their availing themselves of the respite to get up artillery of even greater caliber; the reliance on troops from the North, more than met by reinforcements from the South... I am puzzled to divine the next act of the drama. It will be either another inexplicable evacuation, or the suffocation of this army by the seizure of our communications when least expected. The enemy wishes us to attack. McClellan has proven by fortifications that he is feeble. It is true they will fail if they attack us; but if they do not do that, they will leave enough troops in our front, and crossing the Chickahominy, cut us off from our lines of communication and sustenance....

It was precisely what happened. While McClellan was waiting for "the last man to take his place" Lee brought Jackson from the Shenandoah Valley where he had been mauling the Yankees, and made an audacious move. He took most of his army to the north side of the Chickahominy and grouped it to attack Fitz-John Porter, leaving only a small force to guard the Richmond approaches.

But even as Lee was preparing this maneuver McClellan moved at last. On Wednesday, June 25, orders went to Heintzelman; the command was Forward! In a bleak dawn made uncomfortable by a chilling drizzle Hooker's and Kearny's men shed their knapsacks, filled their cartridge pouches, fixed bayonets and pushed into the gloomy woods. The men were merry despite the miserable weather. Philip's troops cheered as he passed to the fore of the advancing regiments.

"This is the hour for which we have been longing," he announced, doffing his kepi with its scarlet patch, to acknowledge the ovation.

"We'll see you in Richmond, General Phil!" a cocky soldier yelled.

"That's the spirit," Kearny responded.

The Third Corps entered a gloomy wooded area, sloshing ahead over wet and spongy earth. Cannon on both sides opened a brisk fire, but the Rebel guns would not stop Hooker and Kearny; by midafternoon they had gained a mile. Elation spread in the Union ranks—the center of Richmond was now only five miles away. Enemy resistance seemed sporadic; here and there fights broke out, but no large-scale battle developed.

This puzzled Kearny. "Lee has something up his sleeve," he said. "I fear a most unpleasant surprise is in store for us."

He was right. On the afternoon of Thursday, June 26, Lee fell upon Porter's corps near Mechanicsville to open the gory Seven Days of the Peninsular Campaign. Although initially beaten off, the dogged Southern general kept up the attack on the 27th at Gaines' Mill. The fighting was costly on both sides, but Lee drove Porter back.

Had McClellan dared, he would have reinforced Porter and pressed home the attack on Richmond at the same time. Instead, convinced that his army faced a foe 200,000 strong, he was paralyzed by the prospects of failure. He did not know that only 20,000 men under General "Prince John" Magruder blocked the road to Richmond. That small number managed to checkmate the Yankee offensive against the Rebel citadel. As at Yorktown, Magruder put up an epic bluff. In a repeat performance he pretended to have many more troops than were actually present by marching several brigades back and forth to create the illusion of numbers. Officers shouted orders to nonexistent troops, and the Union pickets reported "tremendous activity within the enemy's lines."

This play acting caused Heintzelman to hold up his advance, over the objections of Hooker and Kearny. They sensed a trick. Hooker felt that "Rebel resistance is too spotty for large forces" Kearny argued, "I know Magruder. He's a faker—an actor. Let me call his hand."

His request was not granted. The advance stopped dead, and 70,000 Union troops were stymied by Magruder's 20,000. At the same time McClellan, holed up in Headquarters, lost his nerve. Afraid to send sizeable reinforcements to Porter, for fear his lines south of the River would be broken, neither did he dare strike at Richmond, because disaster threatened on the north bank.

McClellan capitulated to caution. Dig in on both banks, he ordered. Hold Lee in a delaying action and then commence a retreat to a suitable base on the James River, there to regroup, reinforce and re-equip for another offensive at another time. To implement his uninspired decision McClellan sent for his Corps Commanders—Sumner, Keyes, Heintzelman, Porter and Franklin—on the night of June 27, after Gaines' Mill, and announced his purpose. They listened sagely and agreed—retreat was the only reasonable course. The meeting adjourned and the generals departed, but a little later ruddy-cheeked Heintzelman returned with his two Division Commanders, Hooker and Kearny. These warhawks had insisted upon seeing McClellan and had kept at Heintzelman until he consented to go back with them. McClellan met Hooker and Kearny, who were accompanied by several Brigade Commanders, and curtly demanded the reason for their presence.

"The enemy lines around Richmond are thin. They can and must be broken," Kearny bristled. "An order to retreat is wrong! Wrong, sir! I ask permission to attack Magruder at once."

"Denied," McClellan snapped.

The Brigadiers and Hooker backed Kearny. Each was insistent about mounting an attack. "I can go straight into Richmond," Kearny cried, and Hooker assented. "A single division can do it, but to play safe use two divisions— Hooker's and mine," the one-armed General reasoned.

He pointed out the advantages of such a move. Even if McClellan felt the divisions could not hold Richmond, at the very least they would free some 14,000 Union prisoners of war held in Libby Prison and on Belle Island besides "upsetting Lee's plans, shaking the Confederacy to its core, and perhaps capturing some of the enemy's most prominent leaders. It will be a glorious stroke, a brilliant thrust. I can do it and bring my men out of there," Kearny ended with eager confidence.

McClellan was cold and unimpressed. "Nothing has changed, General. The retreat will be made on schedule."

At this juncture Phil lost control. General Hiram Berry, Commander of the Third Brigade, was present and later wrote: "Phil unloosed a broadside. He pitched into McClellan with language so strong that all who heard it expected he would be placed under arrest until a general court-martial could be held. I was certain Kearny would be relieved of his command on the spot."

Nothing that dire took place. McClellan waited for Kearny to calm down and then said nothing in reply. Perhaps he appreciated the merit of the proposal to attack Richmond but simply lacked the moral courage to attempt it; perhaps, wisely, he felt the only way to handle a hothead like Kearny was to let him blow off steam. At any rate, when the tirade ended the officers were politely dismissed to rejoin their commands.

The Union retreat started the following day. The soldiers termed it a "grand skedaddle." As provost guards set fire to huge stores of supplies that could not be moved the nation's hopes—carefully nurtured for nine months—went up in columns of greasy black smoke. The army trudged back through woods and fields, past the hastily buried dead, the charred farmhouses and the old battlefields. A steady rain began falling, and the men marched in sullen silence.

The withdrawal—"a change of base," McClellan called it—became a series of bitter actions with the pursuing enemy. A fight took place at Savage's Station on June 29, and the next day there was an encounter at Glendale (Frazer's Farm) and in White Oak Swamp amid a maze of boggy trails, rotting trees and matted vegetation.

Before entering White Oak Swamp, Kearny insisted that every man in his division must be issued all the extra ammunition he "could carry on his person." Knapsacks and pockets were crammed with cartridges, and personal belongings such as extra clothing were thrown away. "A soldier can fight in soiled underwear but not without bullets," Kearny said.

His foresight was rewarded. An officer in his division flatly stated that "nothing saved the Union army in White Oak Swamp but those extra rounds of ammunition in the Third Division. If it had not been for Phil Kearny our corps would have been destroyed and with it the army...."

Having fought through White Oak, Kearny participated in the ghastly battle of Glendale where the "wailing of the wounded blended into one blood-chilling cry of pain." During this engagement Philip took temporary charge of his old Jersey brigade and led it in a thrilling countercharge. The combat was so fierce that it lasted until well after dark, and as at Solferino three years before, Kearny had a narrow escape from death or capture when he blundered into the enemy lines alone.

Thinking another Union division held the ground to his left, Phil rode there to look at the position. To his dismay he found himself in the midst of a Southern platoon deployed as skirmishers. Fortunately it was already dark and his cloak concealed his uniform. Apparently mistaking Kearny for his own commander, a Rebel officer strode up and asked, "My men are all in position, sir. What shall I do now?"

"Do as I have always directed you to do in such a situation, you fool!" Phil roared, wheeling his horse and riding away.

Once out of effective range, Kearny turned in the saddle and called back, "Good-bye, Rebels! I'll see you all in Hell!" With a mocking wave he sped off to his own men.

CHAPTER XXIII

By Tuesday, July 1, the Army of the Potomac had reached a slope called Malvern Hill on the James River. Every approach to the high ground was covered by Union artillery. When his division arrived at Malvern Hill, Kearny personally placed the brigades. He made the troops throw up breastworks, even though the men were worn out by the rigorous marching. As he came by to watch the entrenching parties at work a grimy soldier was heard to grumble, "The General has one fault. He thinks everybody's made of cast iron like himself."

Complaining bitterly, the men dug trenches, but when the battle started they did not regret the extra exertion. Few units were as well protected as Kearny's. The position was so strong that Phil turned with satisfaction to a staff member and said, "If the Rebels can drive me out of here, they can rightly call me a stupid Jersey fool."

Malvern Hill was perfectly suited for defense. Union gunboats steamed up the James to support McClellan, while supply vessels laden with small-arms ammunition and heavy-caliber shells were at hand to replenish empty caissons and cartridge belts.

Lee attacked on Wednesday, July 2, and the Yankee gunners had a turkey shoot. Batteries massed hub to hub mowed down the charging Confederate infantry "like a scythe cutting tall grass." Within five minutes Lee lost nearly 5,000 men. The Northern artillery was "the thunderbolt of a furious God." Never before in the war had field guns been so effective.

No troops, however brave, could stand such a pounding, and the Rebels staggered away from Malvern Hill in disorder. "Even after the attacks had ended, our cannonading went on ... shells and bullets of every kind tore through the woods in a ceaseless whirlwind of fury ... The enemy fled from the scene wildly, stumbling through swamps and hollows ... as gunboats and batteries blasted away until late at night ... men with torn and mangled limbs ... and gut-shot horses ... dragged themselves away from that awesome inferno. ..." a chaplain with a Pennsylvania regiment wrote of the fighting.

Rain began to fall at sunset. A mist settled down to eclipse the slopes of the hill on which lay the bodies of so many Confederates. The agonized moans of the wounded merged into a single piteous cry for help. "Horribly injured men crawled about like hideous, red-stained creatures," an observer said.

The battle-weary Yankees dropped to the rain-soaked ground for a brief rest. They were exhausted, but satisfied that a victory had been won. "We've whipped Bobby Lee," exulted a sergeant in Kearny's division as he squinted through the mist and the rain at the confused crowds of Confederates fleeing the murderous artillery.

The anonymous sergeant was right. McClellan's men had indeed beaten Lee. Every private in the Army knew that; you didn't have to be a general to see that the enemy was running.

Only McClellan seemed unaware that he had gained the victory. An order came from Headquarters for a farther retreat to Harrison's Landing near the mouth of the James River about six miles from Malvern Hill. Dispatch riders raced through the driving rain to deliver the order which was received with a mixture of amazement and anger. "Retreat! Never!" a Division Commander in Porter's corps shouted. "It's madness! We can't retreat! We have them on the run!"

His reaction was a general one. Even McClellan's close friend General Fitz-John Porter openly announced that to pull back was a mistake. "A determined advance will take Richmond," he said.

As usual it was Kearny who made the strongest protest. When the courier reached him, Phil read the order to his staff in the pouring rain. In the words of a staff officer, "the General carried on like a madman . . . he cried out that it was criminal for a triumphant army to leave the field to a flying foe. His language grew so intemperate that I tried to calm him, but he would not listen. Never had I seen any man that angry...."

To climax his choleric outburst Kearny slammed his famous kepi into the mud and cried out, "I, Philip Kearny, an old soldier, protest this order for retreat. We ought, instead of retreating, to follow up the enemy and take Richmond. And in full view of all the responsibility of such a declaration I say to you all, such an order can only be prompted by cowardice or treason."

However, Kearny and the other commanders obeyed the unpopular order. The downhearted Army of the Potomac slogged through the rain and mud to Harrison's Landing. The troops filed dejectedly into camp and went about the business of encampment.

Harrison's Landing was an unhealthy place at that time of the year. The temperature rose; mosquitoes swarmed in droves; and men by the score fell ill with malaria. Dysentery, ague, chills, fevers—even typhoid—plagued them.

Philip suffered a grave mental depression. Although anxious to see Agnes, he could not bear to leave his troops. "My poor boys sicken and die on every side of me in this disease-ridden hell hole. They need me more than I need you," he wrote her. "I shall come home on leave when I can do so with an easy conscience."

His own health was affected. At night he lay on his camp bed with chills and fever, yet never gave in to the illness. He forced himself to ride out each morning and visit the troops in the field. Wherever he went the soldiers came running to cheer him. At one time they crowded around him for so long that his progress was delayed and he was forced to issue the following order: "The General commanding this division takes great pleasure in the kind reception given him when he passes among the men ... but prefers ... to be allowed to pass quietly and unobserved ... Immediately after a victorious battle he has no objections to a few hearty cheers...."

Kearny felt that the men were "boxed up like herrings" at Harrison's Landing. But the inactivity gave him a much needed rest despite all the difficulties, and for the first time he was able to express his views on the Negro question—the most controversial issue of the day. Where others equivocated, Kearny spoke out forcefully in a letter to Cortland Parker:

... It is time for us to deprive the enemy of his extraneous engines of war ... There is no more Southern man at heart than myself. I am so from education and association ... but I must speak out about the colored race ... As the blacks are the rural military forces of the South, so they should be indiscriminately received by us, if not seized ... I would not yet arm them, but I would use them to replace whites where possible ... In furtherance of this, instead of the usually twenty pioneers per regiment, I would select fifty muscled blacks, giving them the ax, the pick and the shovel ... but also high military organization ... I would use them as cooks, teamsters and artillery drivers ... I would seek French officers for them, for their peculiar gift over "natives" ... also I should advise some Jamaican sergeants to be recruited ... This idea of black adjuncts to the military awakens nothing inhumane ... It but prevents the slave, runaway or abandoned to us, from becoming a moneyed pressure upon us ... It would eventually prepare them for freedom . . . for surely we do not intend to give them back to their Rebel masters. . . .

He amplified these remarks by suggesting that certain Negroes "of the highest intelligence and zeal" be trained as soldiers and formed into regiments for service on the frontier against hostile Indians, "thus relieving army units now employed on such duty for action against the Confederates."

The days at Harrison's Landing reawakened in him the old belief that he had been mistreated by higher authority and that lesser men were being elevated to more important posts. He was especially bitter that Fitz-John Porter had been given command of a corps, complaining that Porter "never yet won a fight . . . whilst I, the like unknown before in our history, a successful division commander, am left without recognition . . . Be sure if this Army were in the hands of a man likely to save it . . . I would pitch my commission to the winds and serve my country otherwise. . . ."

Philip was speaking and writing out of an irritation evoked by the physical discomfort of his recurring illness. He was also irked by the failure of the Peninsular Campaign, which he had foreseen, and he wanted to strike out at somebody—anybody. When he felt put upon Kearny lashed out—often with no cool, mature thought as to what he was saying.

The interlude at Harrison's Landing did not last long for him. In August, 1862, the Government devised another scheme for capturing Richmond. General John Pope was called in from the West to form the Army of Virginia which would march overland against the Confederate Capital along the route of the Alexandria and Orange Railroad. Pope's army was formed of troops earmarked to defend Washington, plus two corps—Heintzelman's and Fitz-John Porter's—from the Army of the Potomac, which remained on the James River.

Pope was an ill-starred man; he evoked the contempt and hatred of the Army of Virginia from the start by his arrogance and intemperance. The misbegotten Army fought only one major battle; the disastrous Second Bull Run, after losing at Gainesville and Groveton.

By August 30, Lee and Jackson had Pope flying toward Washington, although still issuing bombastic and fallacious statements of victory. Kearny fought magnificently during the trying days. At one point he assailed the left of Jackson's line under General Ambrose P. Hill and almost won, but the foe was too strong. Mounted on his superb black charger Winfield, Kearny looked on as his beaten troops straggled out of the woods. When the Third Michigan emerged with only a handful of survivors he wept. "Oh, my poor Michigan boys, my valiant lads, what have they done to you?" he sobbed.

The Army of Virginia stumbled back, battered and bloodied. Kearny went with them, burning at the humiliating defeat. "Are there only imbeciles to lead us?" he railed.

The withdrawal continued all night, like some hideous nightmare. Cavalrymen slept in the saddle; infantry stumbled on; men collapsed in the mud and were crushed to death by wagon wheels. Male nurses broke into the medical liquor stores and held a raucous drunken orgy. It rained so furiously that creeks overflowed and sleeping men were drowned in roadside ditches.

On September 1, the storm grew worse. Lightning lit the sky and thunder crashed like artillery. Phil Kearny's division formed the rear guard of the shattered army which Stonewall Jackson and Ambrose P. Hill followed closely. At dusk the Yankees turned upon their tormentors near a crossroads called Chantilly.

A battle flared about 5 P.M. amid rain, wind and darkness. Kearny, learning of a break in his line, rushed in a battery to plug the gap and then rode out to survey the situation for himself. He galloped past his own First Brigade, pausing to chat with General David Birney, its Commander.

"I'm going to see what lies ahead," he told Birney, and went on alone despite his subordinate's protests that it was too dangerous.

"The Rebel bullet that can kill me has not yet been molded." Kearny laughed and was soon hidden by sheets of rain.

He galloped straight into the outposts of a Confederate regiment. When he reached the enemy a monstrous lightning bolt illuminated the darkness. The Southerners opened fire, and Philip tried to turn his horse. A single bullet hit him at the base of the spine. He fell from the saddle into a pool of rain water.

General Hill ran to the fallen man. By the light of a lantern he looked at the body. "You've killed Phil Kearny," he gasped. "He deserved a better fate than to die in the mud."

Ironically, almost at the moment when Kearny pitched to the ground Secretary of War Stanton was signing papers promoting him to the rank of Major General. In Washington a rumor was being started that Kearny was to replace McClellan as the Commanding General of the Army of the Potomac.

Death had robbed him of the recognition he craved. But it came in a way that granted at least one of his lifelong wishes. He had died for his country.

BIBLIOGRAPHY

I consulted many books, newspapers, manuscripts, journals, diaries, letters and memoirs in gathering material for *Kearny the Magnificent*. The list is long and exhaustive. I have mentioned below only a few of the works I found the most useful:

Baquet, Camille, *History of the 1st Brigade, New Jersey Volunteers*. Trenton: State of New Jersey, 1910.

Catton, Bruce, *Mr. Lincoln's Army*. New York City: Doubleday, 1951.

de Peyster, John Watts, *Personal and Military History of Philip Kearny*. New York: Rice & Gage, 1869.

de Trobriand, Regis, *Four Years With the Army of the Potomac*. Boston: Tichnor & Co., 1889.

Floyd, Fred C., *History of the 40th (Mozart) Regiment, New York Volunteers*. Boston: F. H. Gilson Co., 1909.

Kearny, Thomas, *General Philip Kearny, Battle Soldier of Five Wars*. New York: Putnam, 1937.

Marks, J. J., Reverend, *The Peninsular Campaign in Virginia*. Philadelphia: Lippincott, 1864.

INDEX

Aachen (Germany), 35
Abd-El-Kader, 69, 70, 73, 76, 78
Alexander II (Tsar of Russia), 140
Alexandria (Va.), 194, 197
Alexandria and Orange Railroad (Va.), 181, 193
Algeria, 69, 72, 80
Algiers, 69, 73
Allessandria (Italy), 143
Army of Northern Virginia, 215
Army of the Potomac, 163, 171, 178, 192, 201, 206, 218, 231
Army of Virginia, 234
Atkinson, Gen. Henry, 62, 89
Atlas Mountains (Algeria), 74
Austria, 142ff.
Avenue de Malignen, 141, 149ff.

Baden-Baden (Germany), 35
Ball's Bluff (Va.), 171, 178

Battery (N.Y.), 21, 22, 41, 59
Bellegrove (N.J.), 17, 133, 138, 172ff.
Berry, Gen. Hiram, 225
Bingham, Pvt. Henry, 196ff.
Birney, General David, 235
Black Hawk (horse), 139
Blida (Algeria), 73, 75
Bône (Algeria), 69
Bougie (Algeria), 69
Bowling Green (N.Y.), 22
Brooklyn, 21
Bullitt, Diana ("Die"), 62-63, 83-84
Bull Run (Va.), first battle of, 161, 168; second battle of, 234
Burke's Station (Va.), 181

California gold rush, 125-126
Camarge (Mexico), 99
Cameron, Simon, 156

INDEX

Canal Street (N.Y.), 41
Carlisle (Pa.), 84
Casey, Gen. Silas, 213
Cass, Lewis, 65, 71
Castiglione (Italy), 144
Catlett's Station (Va.), 193
Cavalry School, Royal (Saumur), 17, 64, 67
Centreville (Va.), 182, 183
Cerro Gordo (Mexico), battle of, 101-102
Chantilly (Va.), 13, 17, 235
Chickahominy River (Va.), 210, 213ff., 219
Churubusco (Mexico), battle of, 103-107
Clark, Col. Bayard, 159, 160
Cogswell, Dr. Joseph G., 35, 39
Cold Spring (N.Y.), 39
Columbia College (N.Y.), 45
Columbia River (Ore.), 129
Constantine (Algeria), 70
Constantine, Dr. Maurice, 24, 30, 34
Couch, Gen. Darius M., 214
Cranberry Lake (N.Y.), 40
Custer, Lt. George A., 181

Debrack, Gen. Pierre, 67
Delancey (family), 40
De Peyster (family), 40
De Peyster, John Watts, 43, 50, 55, 56, 59, 65, 86
duc d'Aumale, 76
duc d'Orléans, 70, 72, 73, 77, 79

East Newark (N.J.), 133
East River (N.Y.), 21
Elderkin, Pvt. Tom, 61

Elm City (ship), 195ff.
Evans Creek (Ore.), battle of, 128
Eustic, Lt. William, 64, 66, 67, 71, 84
Excelsior Brigade, 213

Fairfax Courthouse (Va.), 183
Fair Oaks (Va.), battle of *(see* Seven Pines), 17, 213-215, 217, 218
First *Chasseurs d'Afrique*, 70, 74
First New Jersey Brigade, 14, 160ff., 181, 199
First New Jersey Volunteers, 180, 183, 196
First New York (Lincoln) Cavalry, 159ff., 181, 182
First U.S. Dragoons, 60, 64, 82, 89, 92, 125
Five Points (N.Y.), 50, 120, 123
Fontainebleau (France), 65
Fort Leavenworth (Kan.), 61, 89, 91, 94
Fort Sumter (S.C.), 152
Fourth Avenue (N.Y.), 42, 137
Franklin, General William B., 187ff., 194ff.
Franz Josef (Emperor of Austria), 142, 144

Gaines Mill (Va.), battle of, 223
Gainesville (Va.), battle of, 234
Gansevoort (family), 40
Garita San Antonio Abada (Mexico) *(see* San Antonio Gate), 108
Glendale (Va.), battle of, 225

INDEX

Gouverneur (N.Y.), 24, 48, 83, 135
Grant, Gen. Ulysses S., 175
Groveton (Va.), battle of, 234

Hailesboro (N.Y.), 40
Halstead, O. S., 186
Harrison's Landing (Va.), 230ff.
Hawthorne, Nathaniel, 183
Harney, Col. W. S., 105, 108
Heintzelman, Gen. Samuel P., 200, 211, 221ff., 234
Hell Gate (N.Y.), 30
Hidden, Lt. Harry, 182-183
Highland Academy, 39, 44, 49
Hill, Gen. Ambrose P., 234, 235-236
Hill, Gen. Daniel H., 213
Hooker, Gen. Joseph ("Fighting Joe"), 200, 202, 207, 223ff.
Hudson, Capt. W. L., 133
Hudson River (N.Y.), 21, 22, 42

Jackson, J. C., 160
Jackson, Gen. Thomas ("Stonewall"), 221, 234
James River (Va.), 228
Jameson, Gen. Charles, 202
Jay, Peter Augustus, 47, 59
Jefferson Barracks (Mo.), 61, 62
Jersey City (N.J.), 16
Johnston, Gen. Joseph E., 168, 183, 185, 201, 202, 215

Kearny, Ann (daughter), 115
Kearny, Agnes Maxwell (second wife), 12ff., 141ff., 172, 195, 231

Kearny, Archibald Kennedy (son), 150, 172ff.
Kearny, Diana (daughter), 88
Kearny, Diana Bullitt (first wife), 83, 84, 95, 96, 115, 135, 141
Kearny, Elizabeth Watts (daughter), 117
Kearny, John Watts (son), 95
Kearny Patch, The, 217-218
Kearny, Gen. Philip, funeral of, 13ff., motto of, 15; ride on Tarquin, 32-33; loneliness of as boy, 42, 43ff.; temper of, 49-50; enrolls at Columbia College, 51; mock warfare, 51-52; opinion on cavalry, 53; graduates Columbia, 55; goes to Europe, 55-56; clerks for Peter Jay, 59-60; inherits fortune on death of grandfather, 60; commissioned 2nd Lt., 60; assigned First U.S. Dragoons, 61; does frontier duty, 61; aide-de-camp to General Atkinson, 62; meets Diana Bullitt, 62-63; promoted to 1st Lt., 65; assigned to Saumur, 65; opinion on King Louis Philippe, 65; description of Saumur, 66; gives grand fete, 67-68; applies for duty in Africa, 70; appointed to staff of duc d'Orleans, 70; assigned 1st *Chasseurs*, 70; becomes ill, 72; on Arab atrocities, 73; ordered to join *Chasseurs* in field, 74; describes desert, 74; fights Arabs, 76; complimented by King's

INDEX

son, 76; describes Arab tactics, 76; writes letter on combat, 77; takes part in attack on Mount Mozaia, 77-78; awarded Légion d'honneur, 78; returns to New York, 80; turns down Foreign Legion command, 80-81; letter on father, 81-82; father's death, 82; inherits second fortune, 82; appointed aide to General Macomb, 82; marries Diana Bullitt, 83ff.; given post at War Department, 83-84; voices disappointment, 84; put on staff of General Scott, 85; compared to Scott, 85; attitude towards assignment, 86; daughter Susan born, 87; grief at her death, 87; complains about military future, 88; disagreement with Scott, 89; leaves Scott's staff, 89; reassigned 1st Dragoons at Ft. Leavenworth, 89; Diana refuses to go with him, 89-90; commands Co. F, 1st Dragoons, 91; applies lessons learned in Africa, 92; bored by routine, 92-93; makes reconnaissance in Indian Territory, 93-94; returns to New York and resigns army, 95; rejoins army at outbreak of Mexican War, 96; sent to Springfield, Illinois to recruit and equip troops, 98; meets Abraham Lincoln, 99; Co. F joins regiment, 99; goes to front, 100; is assigned to Vera Cruz operation, 100; his troop escorts Scott into Vera Cruz, 101; in action at Cerro Gordo, 101-102; fights at Churubusco, 104-111; leads charge to San Antonio Gate, 107-110; is wounded in left arm, 111; arm amputated, 111; refuses to resign commission, 115; placed in charge of recruiting in New York City, 116; trouble erupts with wife, 117; wife leaves him, 117; is embittered by treatment accorded by War Department, 117; is honored by Union Club, 118; horsewhips gangster, 121; appalled by New York slums, 122; comments on slum landlords, 123; is stricken with smallpox, 123-124; rejoins 1st Dragoons in California, 125; restores order in goldfields, 125ff.; campaigns against Rogue River Indians, 126-128; resigns commission again, 131; travels around world, 133; returns to Bellegrove, 133; goes to France, 134; attends Emperor Louis Napoleon's reception at Tuileries, 134; meets Agnes Maxwell, 134; feelings about Agnes, 135; seeks divorce from Diana but fails, 135; gives up Agnes, 135; flees to Gouverneur, 136; injured in fall, 136; returns to New York, 137;

INDEX

Agnes acts as his nurse, 137-138; lives with her at Bellegrove, 138ff.; angered at gossip about her, 139-140; takes Agnes to Europe, 140; attends coronation of Russian Tsar, 140; Diana divorces him, 141; marries Agnes, 141; resides in Paris, 141ff.; joins French Army to fight Austria, 143ff.; at battle of Solferino, 144-148; is decorated by French Emperor, 149; Agnes bears Archibald, 150; attitude towards growing crisis in U.S., 150ff.; hears of Civil War, 153; returns with family to New York, 155; is rejected for high command, 156ff.; appointed Colonel of Lincoln Cavalry, 160; receives command of 1st N.J. Brigade, 162; President Lincoln appoints him Brigadier General, 163; takes over Brigade, 163ff.; Kearny's flamboyance, 166-167; holds position closest to enemy, 168; compared to McClellan, 169; on Scott's retirement, 171; Kearny's health, 171-172; son taken ill, 172; death of Archibald and aftermath, 174; differs with McClellan, 175; proposes plan to defeat enemy, 175; deals with looters, 176-177; serenaded by troops, 179-180; leads Brigade out of camp, 181; aide describes Kearny, 181-182; advances towards Manassas, 182-184; occupies Manassas, 184; opinions on capture of Manassas, 184; resentment towards McClellan, 183-184; offered divisional command, 187; refuses it to stay with N.J. Brigade, 188; saluted by troops, 188-189; honored by N.J. legislature, 191-192; irked at delay in advance, 193ff.; reaches Yorktown, 198; accepts divisional command, 199; bids farewell to Brigade, 199-200; at Battle of Williamsburg, 203-205; dislike of McClellan grows, 206; on his role at Williamsburg, 207-208; stories about Kearny, 208-209; within sound of Richmond church bells, 211; pessimistic about future, 212-213; at Battle of Fair Oaks (Seven Pines), 213-215; comment on battle, 216; initiates Kearny Patch, 217-218; advances on Richmond, 221; in Seven Days battles, 222-230; argues with McClellan, 224-225; escapes from enemy, 227; at Malvern Hill, 228-231; outburst against McClellan, 231; at Harrison's Landing, 231-233; position on Negroes, 232; transferred to Army of Virginia; at Second Battle of Bull Run, 234-235; at Chantilly, 235-236; death of, 235-236

INDEX

Kearny, Philip Sr. (father), 23ff., 28, 29, 33, 36ff., 40, 41, 43, 45, 60-61, 93
Kearny, Col. Stephen Watts (uncle), 46-47, 49
Kearny, Susan (daughter), 87
Kearny, Susan Watts (mother), 24, 28, 34
Kearny, Suzanne (daughter), 14
Kearny, Virginia (daughter), 14
Kearny's Bridge (N.Y.), 136
Kips Bay (N.Y.), 21

Lee, Gen. Robert E., 202, 215, 220ff., 229
Le Pays de Bourjoully, Colonel, 74, 75
Lincoln, President Abraham, 99, 162, 163, 211
Lombardy (Italy), 144
Lone Star Republic, The, 96
Longstreet, Gen. James, 214
Louis Napoleon (Emperor of France), 134, 144
Louis Philippe (King of France), 65
Louisville (Ky.), 62, 63
Lucky Three, The, 64, 67, 84

McClellan, Gen. George B. ("The Young Napoleon," "Little Mac"), 168, 171, 175, 176, 180, 183ff., 201, 206-207, 210, 212, 219ff., 230ff.
McReynolds, Col. Alexander T., 106, 162

Macomb, Gen. Alexander, 82, 83ff.
Magenta (Italy), battle of, 144
Magruder, Gen. John B. ("Prince John"), 198, 201-202, 222
Malvern Hill (Va.), battle of, 17, 228-231
Manassas Junction (Va.), 175, 180, 182, 183ff.
Manhattan (N.Y.), 21
Marseilles (France), 72
Maxwell, Agnes, 134, 135, 137ff.
Maxwell, Hugh, 134
Mechanicsville (Va.), battle of, 222
Medeah (Algeria), 74
Mexico City, 14, 101, 102, 144
Michaud, Lt. Commander, 66
Milan (Italy), 143
Mincio River (Italy), 144, 147
Monmouth (horse), 139
Montebello (Italy), battle of, 143
Morgan, Governor Edwin, 157
Morris, General, 144, 147, 148
Moscow (horse), 16, 139
Mount Mozaia (Algeria), 74, 75, 77
Munson's Hill (Va.), 168

Natural Dam (N.Y.), 48
Newark (N.J.), 7, 17, 18
New Orleans (La.), 99
New York City, 16, 21, 22, 80, 83, 155
New York Stock Exchange, 24
North Africa, 69
Northampton (Mass.), 34

INDEX

Olden, Governor Charles S., 161
Olmstead, Frederick Law, 138
Oran (Algeria), 69
Oregon Trace, 94
Oswegatchie River (N.Y.), 40, 48

Paducah (Ky.), 95
Parker, Cortland, 16, 97, 130, 159
Passaic River (N.J.), 10
Peninsular Campaign, 192ff.
Peter (butler), 34
Pierce, Gen. Franklin, 111
Pikes Peak, 94
Pillow, Gen. Floyd, 104, 106
Pinkerton, Allan, 212
Pope, Gen. John, 234
Porter, Gen. Fitz-John, 221ff., 230, 234

Quaker Guns, 183

Rensselaer Falls (N.Y.), 48
Richmond (Va.), 180, 193, 210, 211ff., 219ff., 230
Richville (N.Y.), 48
Rio Grande River, 95
Rives, William, 134
Rocky Mountains, 95
Rogue River Indian War, 126-128
Rose Hill (N.Y.), 42, 45, 51, 59, 81, 95, 137
Round Hill School, 34, 36, 39, 49

St. Lawrence County (N.Y.), 24
St. Petersburg (Russia), 140

Saltille (Mexico), 100
San Antonio Gate (*see* Garita San Antonio Abada), 14, 111
San Francisco (Cal.), 125
Sangster's Station (Va.), 182
San Mateo, Convent of, 104ff.
San Patricio Battalion, 103ff.
Santa Anna, General, 101-102, 106
Sardinia, 142
Saumur (France), 17, 64, 66, 67, 70, 71-72
Savage's Station (Va.), battle of, 225
Schermerhorn (family), 40
Schuyler (family), 40
Scott, Gen. Winfield ("Old Fuss and Feathers"), 45, 84, 86-88, 100, 104-105, 108, 157-158, 171
Second Corps, 202
Second New Jersey Volunteers, 167, 170
Seven Days, Battles of, 222-230
Seven Pines (Va.), battle of (*see* Fair Oaks), 213-215, 217
Shenandoah Valley (Va.), 221
Sioux Indians, 94
Smith, Gen. G. W., 214
Solferino (Italy), battle of, 144-148
Springfield (Ill.), 98
Stanton, Edwin M., 211
Staten Island (N.Y.), 21
Stoneman, Gen. George, 202
Stuart, Gen. J. E. B., 218-219
Sumner, Gen. Edwin V., 202, 215ff.

INDEX

Table Rock (Ore.), battle of, 128
Tarquin (horse), 36-37
Taylor, Gen. Zachary, 100
Tenyah Pass (Algeria), 75, 78
Texas, 95
Thayer, Col. Sylvanus, 45
Third Corps, 13, 200, 203ff.
Third Division, 13, 203ff.
Third New Jersey Volunteers, 170, 184
Third U.S. Dragoons, 106
Trinity Church (N.Y.), 16
Tuileries (Paris), 134ff.
Turner, Lt. Henry, 64, 66, 71, 84
Turtle Bay (N.Y.), 21

Ufford, Cyril, 33
Ufford's Academy (N.Y.), 33
Union Club, 118
U.S.S. *Vincennes,* 133

Valée, Marshal, 70, 172
Van Buren, President Martin, 64
Van Buren's Hotel (N.Y.), 136
Van Rensselaer (family), 40
Vera Cruz (Mexico), 100, 101, 144

Via San Antonio (Mexico), 104ff.
Victor Emmanuel II (King of Sardinia), 142ff.
Villafranca (Italy), 148

Walters, Corp. Alfred, 166
War Department, 83, 115
Washington (D.C.), 83-84, 91, 95, 180, 234
Watson, Rev. John Lee, 44, 46
Watts, John (grandfather), 22ff., 26-28, 35, 36ff., 41, 46ff., 49, 55, 60, 123
Watts, Dr. Robert, 116, 136, 137ff., 172ff.
West Point (N.Y.), 39, 44, 45, 47, 131
White Oak Swamp (Va.), battle of, 17, 225
Whittaker House (Va.), 202
Willard's Hotel (D.C), 180
Williamsburg (Va.), battle of, 17, 202, 214, 215
Winfield (horse), 234

Yorktown (Va.), siege of, 196, 198, 201ff., 220